Englisch

ABSCHLUSS-PRÜFUNGS-TRAINER

Realschulabschluss
Niedersachsen

 Deine Online-Angebote findest du hier:

1. Melde dich auf scook.de an.
2. Gib den unten stehenden Zugangscode in die Box ein.
3. Hab viel Spaß mit den Online-Angeboten.

Dein Zugangscode auf
www.scook.de
7bj5h-fx75z

Die Online-Angebote können dort nach Bestätigung der AGB und Lizenzbedingungen genutzt werden.

Cornelsen

Abschlussprüfungstrainer Englisch
Realschulabschluss | Niedersachsen

Illustrationen
alle Illustrationen: **Karen Donnelly**, Brighton

Fotos
akg-images (S. 44: Fototeca Gilardi); **A.P.L.** (S. 27: New Line Cinema); **Fotolia** (S. 9 oben: xalanx, unten: illustrez-vous; S. 13 oben: Ingo Bartussek; S. 31: Africa Studio; S. 33: gkrphoto; S. 35: Andrei Nekrassov; S. 36 Mitte: kaninstudio, re.: Kar Tr; S. 45: honcharr; S. 52 oben: Rawpixel.com, unten: photoeverywhere; S. 58: ivan kmit; S. 63: Victor Moussa; S. 70 oben: corlaffra); **mauritius images** (S. 18: Photo 12/Alamy Stock Photo; S. 21: Penny Tweedie/Alamy Stock Photo); **Shutterstock** (S. 13 unten: JP WALLET; S. 16: Jeff Whyte; S. 17: Constantin Stanciu; S. 19: essevu; S. 28: Evocation Images; S. 36 li.: Gennady Grechishkin; S. 41: oneinchpunch; S. 43: David Pickett; S. 48: Dragan Jovanovic; S. 50: Photomika-com; S. 54: Ser Borakovskyy; S. 57 oben: SUNDAYUA, unten: Mitch Gunn; S. 61: Nolte Lourens; S. 67: Marsan; S. 70 unten: JavaJunkie; S. 71: Stephen Finn; S. 74: Rawpixel.com; S. 79: Marish)

Erarbeitet von: Gwen Berwick, York; Sydney Thorne, York
In Zusammenarbeit mit der Englischredaktion: Klaus Unger (Projektleitung); Jutta Seuren (verantwortliche Redakteurin); Cornelia Frisse; Nicola Regner
Beratende Mitwirkung: Andrea Rohoff, Hannover
Illustrationen: Karen Donnelly, Brighton
Layout-Konzept: Klein & Halm Grafikdesign, Berlin
Umschlaggestaltung: Agentur Rosendahl, Berlin
Layout und technische Umsetzung: Klein & Halm Grafikdesign, Berlin

www.cornelsen.de

Soweit in diesem Lehrwerk Personen fotografisch abgebildet sind und ihnen von der Redaktion fiktive Namen, Berufe, Dialoge und Ähnliches zugeordnet oder diese Personen in bestimmte Kontexte gesetzt werden, dienen diese Zuordnungen und Darstellungen ausschließlich der Veranschaulichung und dem besseren Verständnis des Inhalts.

1. Auflage, 1. Druck 2017

© 2017 Cornelsen Verlag GmbH, Berlin

Das Werk und seine Teile sind urheberrechtlich geschützt.
Jede Nutzung in anderen als den gesetzlich zugelassenen Fällen bedarf der vorherigen schriftlichen Einwilligung des Verlages.
Hinweis zu den §§ 46, 52 a UrhG: Weder das Werk noch seine Teile dürfen ohne eine solche Einwilligung eingescannt und in ein Netzwerk eingestellt werden.
Dies gilt auch für Intranets von Schulen und sonstigen Bildungseinrichtungen.

Druck: H. Heenemann, Berlin

ISBN 978-3-06-034857-2

PEFC zertifiziert
Dieses Produkt stammt aus nachhaltig bewirtschafteten Wäldern und kontrollierten Quellen.
www.pefc.de

Inhaltsverzeichnis

Vorwort

Was erwartet dich in der Prüfung?	4
Wie arbeitest du mit diesem Heft?	6

Training Section

Sprechen – *Speaking*

1. Ablauf und Bewertung der Prüfung	7
2. Typische Aufgabenformate in Niedersachsen	7
3. Sprechen – *Now you*	12

Hörverstehen – *Listening*

1. Ablauf und Bewertung der Prüfung	14
2. Typische Aufgabenformate in Niedersachsen	14
3. Hörverstehen – *Now you*	17

Leseverstehen – *Reading*

1. Ablauf und Bewertung der Prüfung	20
2. Typische Aufgabenformate in Niedersachsen	20
3. Leseverstehen – *Now you*	24

Sprachmittlung – *Mediating*

1. Ablauf und Bewertung der Prüfung	29
2. Typische Aufgabenformate in Niedersachsen	29

Schreiben – *Writing*

1. Ablauf und Bewertung der Prüfung	34
2. Typische Aufgabenformate in Niedersachsen	34

Musterprüfungen

Musterprüfung 1	41
Musterprüfung 2	54
Musterprüfung 3	67
Übersicht über die Aufgaben zum Hörverstehen	80

Lösungen (als Einleger in der Mitte des Heftes)

Training Section	2
Musterprüfungen	3
Tipps für die Prüfung	8

VORWORT

Was erwartet dich in der Prüfung?

Liebe Schülerin, lieber Schüler,
bald ist es für dich so weit und du legst die mündliche und schriftliche Prüfung für den Realschulabschluss im Fach Englisch ab. Damit du weißt, was auf dich zukommt, wollen wir dir genau erklären, was dich in der Prüfung erwartet und wie du dich optimal vorbereiten kannst.

Die Realschulabschluss-Prüfung Englisch im Überblick

Die Prüfung besteht aus einem mündlichen Teil, der in der Regel 12–15 Minuten dauert und einer schriftlichen Prüfung, die insgesamt 120 Minuten dauert. Zusätzlich erhältst du noch 15 Minuten Auswahlzeit, die du zur Orientierung oder zum Überprüfen deiner Lösungen nutzen kannst.

	Kompetenz	Ausgangstexte und Aufgaben	Zeit	Punkte
mündlicher Prüfungsteil	Speaking	• *Warm up – speaking about yourself* • *Speaking prompts* – Bildbeschreibung (auch Tonaufnahmen oder Gegenstände als Sprechanlass möglich) • *Discussion* (zu zweit oder in der Kleingruppe)	12–15 Minuten	40 Punkte

schriftlicher Prüfungsteil	Listening	• mehrere Tonaufnahmen (Part 1 – Part 4)
		• verschiedene Aufgabenformate:
		  – Auswahlaufgaben (*Multiple choice*) mit Bildern oder Sätzen
		  – Notizen anfertigen (*Note-taking*)
		  – Richtig/Falsch-Aufgaben (*True/False*)
			120 Minuten + 15 Minuten Auswahlzeit	25 Punkte[1]

	Reading	• vier Lesetexte (Part 1 – Part 4)
		• verschiedene Aufgabenformate:
		  – Richtig/Falsch-Aufgaben (*True/False*) mit und ohne Zeilenangaben
		  – Zuordnungsaufgaben (*Matching*)
		  – Auswahlaufgaben (*Multiple choice*)
				25 Punkte

	Mediating	• Sprachmittlung zwischen deutsch- und englischsprachigen Sprechern • Teile eines deutsch- oder englischsprachigen Textes (z.B. Flyer, Broschüre) müssen in die andere Sprache übertragen werden		18 Punkte
	Writing	• zwei Sets zur Auswahl mit zwei bis drei zu verfassenden Texten à 50, 80 oder 120 Wörtern • verschiedene Aufgabenformate und Textsorten wie E-Mail, Artikel, Rezension, Geschichte		25 Punkte

Hilfsmittel in der Prüfung

Während der schriftlichen Prüfung sind zweisprachige Wörterbücher erlaubt, aber wegen der begrenzten Zeit findest du in diesem Heft auch Übungen und Tipps, die dir helfen, unbekannte Wörter und Aussagen zu entschlüsseln. Mach dir gleichzeitig bewusst, dass du nicht jedes einzelne Wort kennen musst, um einen Text in seinen wichtigsten Aussagen zu verstehen.

---

[1] Die Punktezahlen können für alle Bereiche von Jahr zu Jahr leicht variieren.

Mündlicher Teil der Abschlussprüfung

Speaking

Der **erste Teil der Prüfung** ist eine mündliche Prüfung. Normalerweise nehmen zwei bis drei Schüler gleichzeitig an der Prüfung teil. Die Prüfung dauert 12–15 Minuten. Es gibt keine Vorbereitungszeit und Hilfsmittel sind nicht zugelassen.

Die Prüfung hat drei Teile:
1. *Warm up – speaking about yourself:* Fragen und Antworten (1–2 Minuten pro Kandidat)
2. *Speaking prompts:* Du redest über ein Bild, manchmal auch über Gegenstände oder Hörmaterialien (2–3 Minuten pro Kandidat)
3. *Discussion:* Paar- oder Gruppendiskussion von visuellen Materialien (Fotos) o. Ä. (2–4 Minuten pro Kandidat)

Schriftlicher Teil der Abschlussprüfung

Die schriftliche Prüfung besteht aus den vier Teilen **Hörverstehen**, **Leseverstehen**, **Sprachmittlung** und **Schreiben**.

Listening

Dieser erste Teil besteht aus Parts 1–4. Zu Part 1 gibt es mehrere kurze Hörtexte, zu den anderen Parts jeweils einen. Die Hörtexte wirst du immer zweimal hören.
Es gibt unterschiedliche Aufgabenformate, die dir alle aus dem Englischunterricht bekannt sind:
- **Auswahlaufgaben (*Multiple choice*)**: Hier werden dir drei bis vier mögliche Lösungen angeboten und du musst die richtige heraussuchen, indem du das richtige Kästchen ankreuzt.
- **Richtig/Falsch-Aufgaben (*True/False*)**: Bei derartigen Aufgaben musst du entscheiden, ob die vorgegebene Aussage über den Text wahr oder falsch ist.
- **Notizen anfertigen (*Note-taking*)**: Bei diesen Aufgaben machst du dir Notizen, um Informationen zum Text zu ergänzen.

Reading

Der zweite Teil umfasst vier unterschiedlich lange Lesetexte.
Auch hier gibt unterschiedliche dir bekannte Aufgabenformate:
- **Richtig/Falsch-Aufgaben (*True/False*)**: Bei derartigen Aufgaben musst du entscheiden, ob die vorgegebene Aussage über den Text wahr oder falsch ist. Oft musst du auch noch die Zeilenangabe der passenden Textstelle angeben.
- **Zuordnungsaufgaben (*Matching*)**: Bei diesen Aufgaben musst du z. B. Textstellen einer Auswahl an Bildern, Aussagen oder Personen zuordnen.
- **Auswahlaufgaben (*Multiple choice*)**: Hier werden dir drei bis vier mögliche Lösungen angeboten und du musst die richtige heraussuchen, indem du das richtige Kästchen ankreuzt.

Mediating

Im dritten Teil geht es um Sprachmittlung.
Zunächst wird eine Situation beschrieben, in der du zwischen deutsch- und englischsprachigen Sprechern vermittelst. Dabei sollst du nicht Wort für Wort übersetzen, sondern die wichtigen Informationen in deinen eigenen Worten übertragen. Dann liest du einen deutschen oder englischen Text, z.B. eine Informationsbroschüre, und gibst die wichtigsten Punkte, angeleitet durch Fragen, in der anderen Sprache wieder.

Writing

Im vierten und letzten Teil der schriftlichen Prüfung bekommst du zwei Sets mit Aufgaben zum Verfassen von jeweils zwei bis drei schriftlichen Texten zur Auswahl, von denen du dich für eines entscheiden musst. Wenn du dich entschieden hast, musst du zwei bis drei Texte (z.B. E-Mails, Bewertungen, Artikel oder Geschichten) verfassen. Das können kurze Texte (50 Wörter) mit vorgegebenen Stichwörtern (*key words*), aber auch mittlere (80 Wörter) oder längere Texte (120 Wörter) sein.

VORWORT

Wie arbeitest du mit diesem Heft?

In diesem Heft lernst du durch gezielte Übungen, wie du die Aufgaben zu allen Prüfungsteilen bearbeiten kannst. Darüber hinaus bekommst du konkrete Prüfungsbeispiele. Das Heft ist deshalb wie folgt aufgebaut:

Das **erste Kapitel**, die *Training Section*, gliedert sich in die fünf Kompetenzbereiche, die in der zentralen Prüfung abgeprüft werden: **Sprechen**, **Hörverstehen**, **Leseverstehen**, **Sprachmittlung** und **Schreiben**.

Die *Training Section* enthält:
- Hinweise zum Ablauf und zur Bewertung jedes einzelnen Kompetenzbereichs
- Beispiele und Tipps für alle Aufgabenformate, die in der Prüfung vorkommen können, also *Multiple choice*, *True/False* etc.
- zahlreiche Strategien zum Umgang mit typischen Schwierigkeiten, wie z. B. Verständnisproblemen
- vielfältige Aufgaben zum Üben deiner Sprechkompetenz und deines Hör- und Leseverständnisses *(Now you)*.

> **Tipp**
> Blau umrandete Felder markieren Tipps, die dir bei den Aufgaben helfen.

Es empfiehlt sich, die *Training Section* als erstes durchzuarbeiten, und zwar Kompetenzbereich für Kompetenzbereich. So verschaffst du dir einen Überblick darüber, was du schon gut kannst, wo du noch üben solltest und welche Strategien dir dabei helfen.

Das **zweite Kapitel** bietet dir drei komplette **Musterprüfungen**, die jeweils alle fünf Kompetenzbereiche (*Speaking*, *Listening*, *Reading*, *Mediating*, *Writing*) enthalten. Sie sind den Prüfungen der letzten Jahre nachempfunden. Du lernst dadurch Schritt für Schritt die gesamte Prüfungssituation und den Aufbau einer Prüfung kennen.

Wenn du feststellst, dass du mit einem Kompetenzbereich oder einem Aufgabenformat noch Schwierigkeiten hast, gehe zurück in die *Training Section* und wiederhole gezielt die entsprechenden Übungen und Strategien oder nutze die Online-Übungen zu Grammatik und Wortschatz auf www.scook.de.

Die **Tonaufnahmen und Hörtexte** für die *Training Section* und die Musterprüfungen findest du ebenfalls online unter www.scook.de. Das Kopfhörer-Symbol mit Track-Nummer im Heft zeigt dir an, welchen Hörtext du für die Aufgabe anhören musst.

Mit dem **Lösungsteil** in der Mitte des Heftes kannst du deine Ergebnisse überprüfen und – wenn nötig – verbessern.

Nützliche Tipps zur Prüfungsvorbereitung erhältst du auf S. 8 des Lösungsteils.

Nun kannst du zuversichtlich sein, dass du weißt, was in der zentralen Prüfung auf dich zukommt, und dass du die unterschiedlichen Aufgabenstellungen geübt hast und kennst.

> Zusätzlich kannst du dein Grundwissen in den Bereichen Grammatik und Wortschatz mithilfe von Online-Übungen wiederholen und vertiefen. Nutze dazu den Zugangscode auf Seite 1 (www.scook.de).
>
> Ebenfalls online findest du die Tonaufnahmen zu den Höraufgaben als MP3-Downloads, die Hörtexte sowie die Originalprüfungen früherer Jahre mit Lösungen. Nutze dazu ebenfalls den Code von Seite 1.

Viel Spaß beim Training mit diesem Heft und viel Erfolg bei der Prüfung!

Sprechen – *Speaking*

1. Ablauf und Bewertung der Prüfung

Ablauf der mündlichen Prüfung

Normalerweise nehmen zwei Schüler gleichzeitig an der Prüfung teil. Es können auch drei sein. Jeder Kandidat wird aber individuell beurteilt. Über die Zusammensetzung der Prüfungsgruppe wirst du vor der Prüfung informiert.

Die Prüfung wird von zwei Fachkräften geführt. Der Prüfer *(interlocutor)* stellt dir die Aufgaben und steuert die Prüfung; der Protokollant *(assessor)* hört zu und macht Notizen. Beide benoten dich gemeinsam.

Die Prüfung dauert 12–15 Minuten. Es gibt keine Vorbereitungszeit und Hilfsmittel sind nicht zugelassen. Die Prüfung beginnt damit, dass der Prüfer sich und den Protokollanten vorstellt. Es folgen dann die drei Teile der Prüfung:
1. *Warm up – speaking about yourself:* Fragen und Antworten (1–2 Minuten pro Kandidat/in)
2. *Speaking prompts:* eine überwiegend monologische Aufgabe mithilfe von Bildern, aber auch Tonaufnahmen oder Gegenstände sind möglich (2–3 Minuten pro Kandidat/in)
3. *Discussion:* Diskussion unter den Kandidaten von visuellen Materialien o.Ä. (2–4 Minuten pro Kandidat/in)

Bewertung der mündlichen Prüfung

Die mündliche Prüfung ist wichtig. Sie macht ein Drittel deiner Gesamtnote der Abschlussprüfung aus. Deine Note hängt natürlich davon ab, wie gut du die gestellten Aufgaben bewältigst. Dazu tragen zum Beispiel folgende Faktoren bei:
– wie fließend und verständlich du kommunizierst, z. B. mit natürlichen Sprechpausen
– ob du die Initiative ergreifst, viele Beiträge lieferst und dafür sorgst, dass das Gespräch aufrechterhalten wird,
– ob du eine Vielfalt an Wortschatz und Strukturen verwendest,
– deine Aussprache und Satzmelodie.

Fragen zur Klärung und zum Verständnis, soweit sie relevant und auf Englisch sind, werden positiv bewertet. Überlange Pausen werden dagegen negativ bewertet.

2. Typische Aufgabenformate in Niedersachsen

In diesem Kapitel lernst du die typischen Aufgabenformate kennen, die dich bei der mündlichen Prüfung erwarten. Die blauen Kästen enthalten nützliche Strategien, wie du mit häufigen Schwierigkeiten umgehen kannst.
Wie kannst du diese Aufgaben am besten bearbeiten?
Du könntest z.B.
– zu Hause alleine arbeiten und, falls möglich, deine Stimme aufnehmen,
– in der Schule mit einem Partner oder einer Partnerin zusammenarbeiten; erst jede(r) für sich, dann zur gegenseitigen Hilfe miteinander,
– die Tipps, die du am nützlichsten findest, unterstreichen,
– …

TRAINING SECTION: Speaking

Part 1: Warm up

Speaking about yourself

a) Questions + short answers
   Answer these questions about yourself.
   1 Hello. How are you today?
   2 What's your name?
   3 How do you spell your first name? /
     … your last name?
   4 Where do you live?
   5 How long have you been living there?
   6 What's your favourite food? /
     … your favourite school subject?

> **Tipp**
> Teil 1 dauert 1–2 Minuten und beginnt mit ein paar Fragen, die kurz beantwortet werden können. Aber auch kurze Antworten sollen natürlich klingen, z. B. auf die Frage:
> – *How long have you been living here?*
> besser: – *Oh, about six years or so.*
> als bloß: – *Six years.*

b) Questions + longer answers

   Give longer answers to these questions.

1 **Tell me something about your home town. Do you like it here?**

> **Tipp**
> – Auflistungen von Orten (*cafes, shops, cinemas, …*) bekommen nur wenige Punkte. Verwende eher Strukturen wie z.B. *There are some nice cafes not too far from my house. I can easily take a bus to the shops.*
> – Begründe deine Meinung: Statt nur *Yes* oder *No* verwende immer *Yes, because …* oder *No, but …*

2 **What do you like doing in your free time?**

> **Tipp**
> – Du bekommst Punkte dafür, dass du das Gespräch aufrechterhältst. Erzähle also zwei bis drei Einzelheiten zu jeder Freizeitaktivität.
> Nicht: *I play football. I meet my friends. I listen to …*
> Sondern: *I play football on Tuesday afternoon for a club in town. I've played in the same club for two years, and I really like the people there. I also often meet my friends, for example after school we …*

3 **What kind of animal would make a good pet?**

> **Tipp**
> – Begründe deine Meinung, z.B.:
> *Dogs can be really good pets because … But if you live in a small flat, it would be difficult because …*
> – Greife auf Beispiele zurück, z.B.:
> *Rats can be really good pets. That's surprising, isn't it? But I have a friend who has a rat, and she loves it because …*

4 **What are you going to do in your next holidays?**

> **Tipp**
> – Vorsicht bei Fragen, die im *simple past* oder (wie hier) *going to*-future gestellt werden. Sie müssen dann auch in der Vergangenheit oder im Futur beantwortet werden.
> – *Well, I'm not sure. I think I'm going to …, but maybe we'll …*

Part 2: Speaking prompts

Jeder Kandidat bekommt einen eigenen Sprechanlass, wahrscheinlich ein Foto. Du sprichst 2–3 Minuten lang über deinen Sprechanlass und hörst still zu, während dein/e Mitschüler/in ebenfalls 2–3 Minuten lang über sein oder ihr Thema spricht.

TRAINING SECTION: Speaking

a) Picture prompt

Talk about the picture.
— What can you see?
— Talk about their feelings.

Tipp

Du beginnst damit, dass du das Bild beschreibst. Hier zählen ein großer Wortschatz und die Verwendung einer Vielfalt von Strukturen. Die Verben sind meist im *present progressive*, z.B.
— *I can see two young people who are carrying very heavy rucksacks.*

Du kannst spekulieren, was sie gerade gemacht haben bzw. bald machen werden, z.B.
— *Maybe they spent last night in a tent, so I imagine that they didn't sleep much.*
— *I think they are looking forward to a rest.*

Vergiss nicht, über ihre Gefühle zu reden, z.B.
— *I'm sure they are really tired and thirsty, but maybe they feel proud that they have walked so far.*

Du kannst auch sagen, ob gerne dabei wärst, z.B.
— *I wouldn't want to be with them because if there's one thing I can't stand, it's hiking!*

b) Object prompt

Talk about the object.
— Do you like this sort of food?
— Why is this sort of food popular?

Tipp

Wenn du das Wort für den Gegenstand im Bild vergessen hast, kannst du ihn umschreiben, z. B.:
— *I really love this kind of food. I know that food like this isn't healthy, but ...*

Du bekommst Punkte dafür, dass du das Gespräch aufrechterhältst. Gehe in deinen Antworten also immer über die Fragen hinaus, z.B.
— *I like crisps, especially when I'm hungry between lessons. I know they're not very good for me, but ...*

Wenn du zu früh aufhörst zu reden, wird dir der Prüfer Zusatzfragen stellen, z.B.
— *What do you think of labelling healthy food like apples with a green badge and unhealthy food like crisps with a red one?*
— *Discuss the pros and cons of fast food versus fresh food.*

Das ist oft viel schwieriger, weil der Prüfer das Thema bestimmt, ob du den notwendigen Wortschatz kennst oder nicht. Das kannst du vermeiden, wenn du selber weitersprichst☺!

TRAINING SECTION: Speaking

c) Sound sequence audio prompt

Hier besteht der Sprechanlass aus Hörsequenzen von aufgenommenen Stimmen oder Geräuschen, die dir vorgespielt werden.

Listen to the sounds.
Then talk about what you hear.
 – What did you hear?
 – What do you think happened?

Tipp

Hier geht es oft um Vermutungen, also helfen Ausdrücke wie z. B.:
 – *I think I heard somebody who …*
 – *I'm not absolutely sure, but it sounded to me like …*

Du kannst deiner Fantasie freien Lauf lassen, z.B.
 – *Somebody left his or her house in a hurry and ran for the bus. Maybe it was somebody who was going to an interview for a job or a girl who was going on a date with a new boyfriend.*

Du kannst spekulieren, was zuvor passiert ist bzw. was nachher passieren wird.
 – *The young woman who missed her bus probably overslept.*

Part 3: Discussion

Jeder der zwei oder drei Kandidaten bekommt einen Redeanlass, z. B. eine Karte mit Wörtern oder Bildern zu einem Thema. Eure Aufgabe besteht darin, eine Diskussion zum Thema zu beginnen und aufrechtzuerhalten. Jeder Kandidat soll insgesamt 2–4 Minuten lang zu Wort kommen.
Der Prüfer kann nachhelfen, wenn das Gespräch stockt, oder wenn ein Kandidat nicht genug zu Wort kommt.

a) Word prompts

In this part of the test you are talking to each other. Imagine that your town has money to spend on good projects for young people.
Talk to each other about what projects the town should support.
On your cards, there are some ideas, but you can suggest other things too.
Talk about how useful these projects would be for young people in your town and try to agree about the three most useful ones. You have about five minutes. Start when you are ready.

Candidate 1
- More night buses
- A new sports centre
- Free job training for unemployed people
- More cycle tracks
- Free wifi everywhere
- Any more ideas?

Candidate 2
- A hostel for homeless people
- A new swimming pool
- Free bus travel for people under 20
- A free laptop for all students
- A youth club open every evening
- Any more ideas?

Tipp

Formuliere Argumente:
 – *I really think the town should …*
 – *If the town wants to help as many people as possible, it should …*

Setze Prioritäten:
 – *So what do you think should be top of our list? And what should be second?*
 – *In my opinion the most important project of all is …*

Bringe deine eigenen Ideen in die Diskussion:
 – *It's not on my card, but I think free classes in acrobatics would be a good idea. It's fun and would help to keep more young people fit and healthy.*
  • Höre deinem Partner zu und schaue ihn dabei an.
  • Stelle ihm Fragen und zeige Interesse an seinen Antworten.
  • Lass deinen Partner zu Wort kommen und beantworte seine Fragen.
 – *Yes, I agree that we should …, but I think …*
 – *That's a good point. I hadn't thought of that. So maybe we should put … at the top of our list instead.*

Kommt zu einem gemeinsamen Schluss:
 – *OK, so what have we agreed so far? Should we put … at the top of our list? And should we include …?*
 – *We've agreed on two projects, but we need a third one. What do you suggest?*

b) Picture prompts

In this part of the test you are talking to each other.
Imagine that you and your partner are going to go on a three-day hike.
- You are going to spend the night in a tent.
- You are going to take a tent, rucksacks, warm clothes, phones, money, food and washing things.

Talk to each other about what other things you should take.
You'll find some ideas on your cards, but you can suggest other things too.
Talk about how useful these things would be for your hike and try to agree on the five most useful ones.
You have about five minutes.
Start when you are ready.

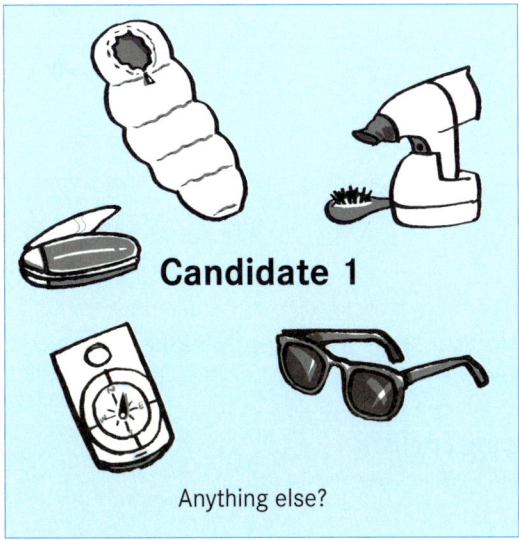

Tipp

FAQs (frequently asked questions)

Q1 Gibt es irgendwo eine Liste von nützlichen Ausdrücken, die ich verwenden könnte?
A1 Na klar! Viele Ausdrücke von Abschnitt **3a)** kannst du auch hier verwenden.

Q2 Was mache ich, wenn ich das Wort für ein Bild nicht kenne?
A2 Keine Panik. Denke an Umformulierungen, z.B. *Maybe we should take these things to make a fire ...* (= Streichhölzer)
Du kannst auch deinen Partner um Hilfe bitten, z.B.: *We need this thing to help us see at night, when it's dark ... Do you know the word?* (= Taschenlampe)
Und übrigens: Wenn du stattdessen deine eigenen Ideen in die Diskussion einbringst, dann brauchst du „das Ding" gar nicht zu erwähnen!

Q3 Wir reden erst seit einer Minute und haben uns schon auf fünf Sachen geeinigt! Wie können wir die Diskussion auf 2–4 Minuten verlängern?
A3 Probiert es noch einmal, und sagt auch etwas zu den Gegenständen, die ihr **nicht** nehmen wollt.
 – *We don't need a compass.*
 – *Really? It could be useful if we got lost. I can't read a map very well, and it could get foggy!*
 – *That's true, but I have a compass on my smartphone. So if we get lost, we can use that.*

Q4 Ich rede die ganze Zeit und mein Partner sagt fast nichts. Das ist nicht fair – ich mache die ganze Arbeit! Wie kann ich das vermeiden?
A4 Stelle deinem Partner Fragen und warte, bis er antwortet.
 – *Should we take a penknife? What do you think?*

TRAINING SECTION: Speaking

3. Sprechen – *Now you*

Hier bekommst du die Möglichkeit, die Strategien, die du auf den letzten Seiten gelernt hast, bei ausgewählten Aufgaben zum Sprechen umzusetzen. Arbeite mit einem Partner/einer Partnerin zusammen.

Part 1 – Speaking about yourself

1 Stelle deinem Partner/deiner Partnerin fünf Fragen.
  Beantworte dann fünf Fragen deines Partners oder deiner Partnerin.

> What's your name and how do you spell it?

> What did you do yesterday evening?

> What do you usually eat for lunch?

> How much sport do you do each week?

> How are you today?

> How do you come to school every day?

> Where do you live?

> What's your favourite school subject?

> How do you spell your family name?

> How long have you been learning English?

2 Gebt euch keine Vorbereitungszeit.
  – Partner/in A spielt den Prüfer und stellt Partner/in B eine Frage (und evtl. auch Zusatzfragen).
  – Die längere Antwort soll 1–2 Minuten dauern. Sollte sie kürzer sein, kannst du als Prüfer/in Zusatzfragen stellen.
  – Tauscht die Rollen und stellt einander eine andere Frage.

1
> **Please tell me something about the place where you live.**
> *house/flat? garden? rooms? own room? people you live with? brothers and sisters? family? pet? village/town? activities/facilities/tourist attractions?*

2
> **Can you tell me something about this school?**
> *favourite subjects? activities/sports? teachers? atmosphere? school trips? canteen/kiosk?*

3
> **Please talk about the activities that you do in your free time.**
> *hobbies/sports? films/TV/media? youth club? help at home? disco/parties? friends? shopping?*

4
> **Can you please tell me about what you usually do in your summer holidays?**
> *family visits? trips with friends or family? at home or abroad? visitors to your home? boring or exciting?*

Part 2 – Picture prompts

Arbeitet zu zweit. Gebt euch keine Vorbereitungszeit.
Partner/in A spielt den Prüfer und stellt Partner/in B eine Aufgabe.
Die Antwort soll 2–3 Minuten dauern. Sollte sie kürzer sein, kannst du als Prüfer/in Zusatzfragen stellen.
Tauscht die Rollen mit einer anderen Aufgabe.

Talk about the picture.
— What can you see?
— Talk about the people's feelings.

Zusatzfragen
Where are the people?
How are they feeling?
Are you scared of big crowds?

Talk about the picture.
— What can you see?
— Talk about the people's feelings.

Zusatzfragen
What has the older person just done beforehand?
How are the two people feeling?
Do you help people near you?

Part 3 – Discussion

In this part of the test you are talking to each other.
Imagine that there are plans to build a new airport about 10 kilometres away from your school (if you have an airport 10 km from your school, discuss plans for a new terminal).
Talk to each other about possible advantages and downsides of this plan.
On your cards there are some ideas but you can suggest other things too.
After discussing the pros and cons of a new airport, try to agree whether you think it is a good idea or not.
You have about five minutes.
Start when you are ready.

Candidate 1	Candidate 2
More (weekend) jobs	Good/bad for environment?
Easy to fly abroad	Noise of lorries and building work
Noise of planes	Easier family visits to you
Destroy some houses?	Tourists good for town economy
More traffic on the roads	New roads good for town?
Any more ideas?	Any more ideas?

TRAINING SECTION: Listening

Hörverstehen – *Listening*

1. Ablauf und Bewertung der Prüfung

Die Prüfung

Die geschriebene Prüfung besteht aus **Hörverstehen, Leseverstehen, Mediating** und **Schreiben**. Für alle Teile zusammen hast du 120 Minuten Zeit. Zusätzlich erhältst du 15 Minuten Auswahlzeit, die du verwenden kannst, wie du willst – du kannst diese Zeit z. B. nutzen, um dir einen Überblick über die Aufgaben zu verschaffen oder um deine Lösungen nochmals zu überprüfen. Wenn du mit dem Hörverstehen und Leseverstehen früher fertig bist, hast du entsprechend mehr Zeit für Mediating und Schreiben.

Ablauf beim Hörverstehen

Beim **Hörverstehen hörst du zunächst mehrere Dialoge**. Dazu gibt es Auswahlaufgaben *(multiple choice)* mit Bildern und Sätzen. Dann hörst du einen oder zwei monologische Texte und machst dazu Notizen, um Informationen zum Text zu vervollständigen. Und schließlich gibt es noch einen Hörtext, den du mit einer *Richtig/Falsch*-Aufgabe bearbeitest.

Du hörst alle Hörtexte zweimal. Du hast zunächst 30 Sekunden Zeit, um die Aufgaben zu lesen. Dann hörst du den Hörtext zum ersten Mal. Du bearbeitest die Aufgaben und hörst anschließend den Hörtext noch ein zweites Mal. Dies ist das Vorgehen bei allen Texten der Prüfung.

Bewertung beim Hörverstehen

Ein zweisprachiges oder elektronisches Wörterbuch ist erlaubt.

Du brauchst aber keine Angst vor Grammatik- oder Rechtschreibfehlern in deinen Antworten zu haben. Solange man versteht, was du geschrieben hast, gehen sie in diesem Prüfungsteil nicht in die Bewertung ein. Das Hörverstehen macht ungefähr 18 % deiner Gesamtnote aus.

2. Typische Aufgabenformate in Niedersachsen

In diesem Kapitel lernst du die typischen Aufgabenformate kennen, die dich bei der Abschlussprüfung im Bereich Hörverstehen erwarten. Die blauen Kästen enthalten nützliche Strategien, wie du mit häufigen Schwierigkeiten umgehen kannst.

Part 1 – Auswahlaufgaben *(Multiple choice)* mit Bildern

Olivia and Dad

Before you listen, read and do the task in the tip box.

> **Tipp**
>
> In der Prüfung hörst du eine Reihe von kurzen Dialogen. Du musst zu jedem Dialog das richtige Bild ankreuzen.
> - Sieh dir die Bilder an, <u>bevor</u> du beginnst, zuzuhören.
> - Überlege, wie das Dargestellte auf Englisch heißen könnte.
> - Versuche zu erraten, welche Wörter du bei jedem Bild im Hörtext hören wirst. In diesem Beispiel: Bild **A**: *swimming, pool*   Bild **B**: ?   Bild **C**: ?

TRAINING SECTION: Listening

 What are they planning to do?

A ☐

B ☐

C ☒

Now do the exam task.

- You will hear a short conversation.
- You will hear the conversation twice.
- Choose the correct picture and put a tick (✓) in the box below it.

Tipp

- Fokussiere auf die Wörter im Dialog, die für die Aufgabe wichtig sind. Wiederhole diese Wörter leise im Kopf, während du das richtige Bild auswählst.
- Wenn du nicht gleich auf die richtige Antwort kommst, weil du manche Wörter im Text nicht verstanden hast, kannst du das Ausschlussverfahren anwenden.
- Du kannst auch versuchen, die unbekannten Wörter aufzuschreiben. Wenn du später Zeit hast, kannst du dann die Wörter im Wörterbuch nachschlagen (aber beantworte zuerst alle anderen Fragen).

Part 2 – Auswahlaufgaben *(Multiple choice)* mit Sätzen

First read the questions and the tip boxes, and do the tasks in the tip boxes.
Then do the exam task.

Tim's visit to Krakow

- You will hear Tim and his friend Sinan talking about Tim's visit to Krakow.
- For questions 1–4 tick (✓) the correct box A, B or C.
- You will hear the conversation twice.

1. How did Tim travel to Krakow?
   a) ☐ by train
   b) ☒ by plane
   c) ☐ by car

Tipp

Bei *Multiple choice*-Aufgaben hörst du oft nicht genau das gleiche Wort in a), b) oder c), sondern Hinweise, die zum Thema gehören.
Beispiel:
– Statt *by train* hörst du vielleicht *at the station*.
– Statt *by car* hörst du vielleicht *we drove*.
Welche Wörter oder Ausdrücke könnten dich auf *by plane* bringen?

2. Where did Tim stay in Krakow?
   a) ☐ with a member of his family in a village
   b) ☐ with a friend in the town centre
   c) ☒ in town, but a little way out of the city centre

Tipp

Es kann es sein, dass du ein Wort im Hörtext nicht kennst – hier zum Beispiel *suburb*.
Trotzdem kannst du oft auf die richtige Lösung kommen, wenn du das Ausschlussverfahren anwendest:
– Du wirst hören, dass Tim seine Unterkunft per Internet gebucht hat. Welche zwei Möglichkeiten fallen dadurch wohl aus?

15

TRAINING SECTION: Listening

3 What places did Tim like in Krakow?

a) ☒ places with few tourists

b) ☐ the main tourist sites

c) ☐ places with not too many people

> **Tipp**
>
> **Vorsicht bei identischen Wörtern** in Hörtext und Aufgabe! Sie deuten nicht unbedingt auf die richtige Lösung.
> Beispiel: Im Hörtext und in Antwort b) kommt *main tourist sites* vor. Ist b) folglich die richtige Lösung? Nein! Wie könnte das zu erklären sein?

4 How did Tim make himself understood? With English and …

a) ☐ no Polish, but lots of smiles.

b) ☒ a little Polish, and by making signs.

c) ☐ Polish learnt at school.

> **Tipp**
>
> Bei *Multiple choice*-Aufgaben werden einzelne Wörter aus dem Hörtext häufig ersetzt durch:
> - **Synonyme** (Wörter und Ausdrücke mit ähnlicher Bedeutung, wie *great – wonderful*)
> - **Antonyme** (Wörter und Ausdrücke mit gegensätzlicher Bedeutung, wie *great – awful / not great at all*)
>
> Dieses Wissen kann dir helfen, die richtige Lösung zu finden, z.B. hier:
> Zu *a little Polish* in b) gibt es im Dialog ein Synonym: *a few words* of Polish.
> Im Hörtext gibt es auch ein Synonym zu *making signs*. Welcher Ausdruck könnte es sein?
> Zu *learnt at school* in c) gibt es im Hörtext ein Antonym. Wie lautet es?

Part 3 – Notizen anfertigen *(Note-taking)*

Calgary's skyways (Part 1)

You have found a podcast to help you prepare a presentation about the skyway network in Calgary, a city in Western Canada, for your English class at school.

- Listen to the podcast.
- Complete the notes by filling the gaps 1–5.
- Listen carefully.
- You will hear the recording twice.

Overhead pedestrian passage in Calgary

Length:	1 _18_ kilometres
Height above ground:	2 _4,5_ metres
Called the +15 because …	3 _15 fets_
Advantages for pedestrians:	4a) _Rain, cold_
	b) _Safe_
Disadvantage for the town:	5 _Steet empty_

> **Tipp**
>
> Hier geht es um Zahlen. Achte auf die Maße: Geht es um *miles* oder *kilometres*, um *feet* oder *metres*?

> **Tipp**
>
> - Hier kannst du in deinen eigenen Worten antworten. Du brauchst nicht Wort für Wort aus dem Hörtext zu zitieren.
> - Fragen mit zwei Lücken (hier bei 4) sind zwei Punkte wert. Gib also zwei verschiedene Antworten.

Part 4 – Richtig/Falsch-Aufgaben *(True/False)*

Calgary's skyways (Part 2)

You will now hear part of a radio interview on the Calgary Skyways in Canada.

- Decide whether each sentence is true or false.
- Put a tick (✓) in the correct box 'true' or 'false'.
- You will hear the programme twice.

Tipp
- Vorsicht bei Sätzen mit Zahlen: Achte nicht nur auf die Zahl, sondern auch auf den Rest des Satzes, z. B. *every weekend* in Satz 1.
- Achte auch auf **Synonyme**, z. B. *a native of* im Hörtext = *born in* in Satz 2.

		true	false
1	Over 22,000 people use the busiest bridge every weekend.		✗
2	Harold Hanen was born in Calgary.	✗	
3	He did some of his studies outside Canada.	✗	

3. Hörverstehen – *Now you*

In diesem Kapitel kannst du die Strategien, die du auf den letzten Seiten kennen gelernt hast, bei ausgewählten Aufgaben zum Hörverstehen gezielt üben. Grundlage dafür sind ein Dialog über ein Radrennen in Yorkshire sowie ein Radio-Interview über die jamaikanische Reggae-Legende Bob Marley.

Auswahlaufgaben *(Multiple choice)*

The Tour de Yorkshire

Sarah from Ireland and Mo from Yorkshire are talking about a cycling race in Yorkshire. You will hear their telephone conversation.

- First read the tasks.
- Then listen to the dialogue.
- While you are listening, tick the correct box.
- At the end you will hear the dialogue again.

Yellow bicycle on the city walls of York, 2014

1 In 2014 the *Tour de France* cycling race ...

   a) ☐ began in France and came to Yorkshire.

   b) ☐ went through other countries and then came to Yorkshire.

   c) ✗ began in Yorkshire.

TRAINING SECTION: Listening

2 During the stages of the race in Yorkshire ...
   a) ☐ cycling fans rode yellow bicycles on the sides of the roads used by the race.
   b) ☐ people bought lots of yellow bicycles.
   c) ☒ there were old yellow bicycles on the sides of the roads used by the race.

3 The organizers of the *Tour de France* ...
   a) ☐ planned for large crowds.
   b) ☒ did not expect the enthusiastic reaction from people in Yorkshire.
   c) ☐ hoped that many people would join the cyclists.

4 The *Tour de France* ...
   a) ☐ was in Yorkshire for 21 days.
   b) ☒ left people in Yorkshire wanting to see more cycling races.
   c) ☐ went from Yorkshire directly on to France.

5 The *Tour de Yorkshire* cycling race ...
   a) ☒ includes hills that are difficult even for experienced cyclists.
   b) ☐ uses wide roads to allow for big groups of cyclists to pass through.
   c) ☐ has become a very popular off-road race.

Richtig/Falsch-Aufgaben *(True/False)*

🎧 *Bob Marley*
7
Radio presenter Joshua Needham is talking to Reggae expert Gwen Devlin about the Jamaican singer-songwriter Bob Marley. Listen to the interview.

- Decide whether each sentence is true or false.
- Put a tick (✓) in the correct box 'true' or 'false'.
- You will hear the interview twice.

Bob Marley (1945–1981)

		true	false
1	Bob Marley's dad was much older than his wife.	☒	☐
2	Kingston was an important place for Bob Marley's musical life.	☒	☐
3	Fans agree that Bob Marley's early song *Simmer Down* was his best song.	☐	☒
4	In a shooting incident, Marley's wife was killed.	☒	☐
5	In England, Bob Marley became a songwriter.	☒	☐
6	Bob Marley was a controversial figure because he took drugs.	☐	☐
7	When Bob Marley discovered he had cancer, he flew straight back to Jamaica.	☐	☒
8	Bob Marley died in Jamaica.	☐	☒

TRAINING SECTION: Listening

Notizen anfertigen *(Note-taking)*

 Top of the Rock

You are on a visit to New York City, and you hear this radio advert for the *Top of the Rock* Observation Deck.

- *Listen to the advert.*
- *Complete the notes by filling the gaps 1–6.*
- *You will hear the recording twice.*
- *The first question is an example.*

View from *Top of the Rock* Observation Desk

Number of floors up:	0	*70*
Great views of buildings and …	1	
Opens at:	2	8 am
Advantage of online tickets:	3	
Price for 16 year olds:	4	
Advantage of Sun and Stars tickets:	5	
Tip for night visits:	6	

19

TRAINING SECTION: Reading

Leseverstehen – *Reading*

1. Ablauf und Bewertung der Prüfung

Die Prüfung

Die schriftliche Prüfung besteht aus **Hörverstehen, Leseverstehen, Mediating** und **Schreiben**. Für das Ganze hast du 120 Minuten Zeit. Zusätzlich erhältst du 15 Minuten Auswahlzeit, in der du dich für ein Writing Set entscheiden kannst.

Ablauf beim Leseverstehen

In diesem Teil der Prüfung liest du zunächst ein paar kurze Texte (z. B. Anzeigen) und bearbeitest dann Aufgaben zum Text. Auf *True/False*-Fragen folgen eine Zuordnungsaufgabe *(Matching)*, eine Auswahlaufgabe *(Multiple choice)* und noch ein Text, oft ein Sachtext, mit *True/False*-Fragen, zu denen du dieses Mal aber auch die Zeilenangaben ergänzt.

Bewertung beim Leseverstehen

Auch beim Leseverstehen ist ein zweisprachiges oder elektronisches Wörterbuch erlaubt.
Bei deinen Antworten werden Rechtschreib- und Grammatikfehler nur dann bewertet, wenn man nicht mehr verstehen kann, was du geschrieben hast. Das Leseverstehen macht ungefähr ein Drittel der schriftlichen Abschlussprüfung und 18% deiner Gesamtnote aus.

2. Typische Aufgabenformate in Niedersachsen

Im Folgenden lernst du die typischen Textsorten und Aufgabentypen kennen, die dich bei der Abschlussprüfung im Bereich Leseverstehen erwarten. Die Aufgaben beziehen sich auf einen Sachtext *(Australia's Stolen Generations)*, verschiedene Urlaubsanzeigen *(Activities for Karen, Jack and Olivia)* und einen Dialog *(Kasun)*.
Die Lesetexte sind hier teilweise kürzer als in der Abschlussprüfung.
Die Tipp-Kästen enthalten nützliche Strategien, um mit typischen Schwierigkeiten umzugehen.

Auswahlaufgaben *(Multiple choice)*

Australia's Stolen Generations

The following texts are from a museum about Aboriginal people in Australia.

- *First read the text.*
- *Then tick (✓) the correct statement.*
- *There is only one correct solution per statement.*

Tipp

Bei *Multiple choice*-Aufgaben werden einzelne Wörter aus dem Lesetext oft ersetzt durch:
- **Synonyme** (Wörter mit ähnlicher Bedeutung, wie *pretty – beautiful*)
- **Antonyme** (Wörter mit gegensätzlicher Bedeutung, wie *pretty – ugly*)

Dieses Wissen kann dir helfen, die richtige Lösung zu finden, z.B. hier:
- Wie lautet das Antonym im Text zu *forced to stay* in **1c)**?

TRAINING SECTION: Reading

In the mid-20th century the Australian government adopted a new policy known as the indigenous child removal policy and officials began to take Aboriginal children away from their mothers and fathers, usually by force.

This was the fate of over 250,000 Aboriginal children, some say as many as 500,000, who had to leave their homes.

The children from Aboriginal families were housed in new English-speaking homes where they were not allowed to speak their own language. And they were given the typical foods of white Australians, even though they weren't used to it.

Aboriginal child in Australia

1 Thousands of Aboriginal Australian children …

   a) ☐ died of disease.
   b) ☐ were removed from their parents.
   c) ☐ were forced to stay with their parents.

2 In their new homes the Aboriginal children had to …

   a) ☐ eat food that was new to them.
   b) ☐ give food to white Australians.
   c) ☐ speak their own language.

Tipp

Ein **Aktivsatz** im Text kann zu einem **Passivsatz** bei den Aufgaben werden (oder umgekehrt):

bei den Aufgaben:	im Text:
Passiv	**Aktiv**
1b) … children were removed …	… began to _____ children away …
Aktiv	**Passiv**
2a) … the children had to eat food …	… they were _____ foods …

Tipp

Vorsicht bei identischen Wörtern in Lesetext und Aufgabe! Im Lesetext kommt *speak their own language* vor – wie in Satz **2c)**. **2c)** ist aber nicht die richtige Lösung! Warum nicht?

Richtig/falsch-Aufgaben *(True/False)*

- *Read the text below. Then read the statement.*
- *Decide whether the statement is true or false.*
- *Then tick (✓) the correct box.*

The parents were not told where their children were, and the children were not allowed to have any contact with their parents. The result was that all contact with their families, their language, their music and their way of life was broken off.

Tipp

Achte auf **Sammelbegriffe**, die stellvertretend für eine Reihe von Beispielen verwendet werden können:

im Text:	deine Antwort:
families, language, music, way of life	Sammelbegriff: Culture .

	true	false
In time, Aboriginal Australians lost touch with their culture.	☐	☐

21

TRAINING SECTION: Reading

Zuordnungsaufgaben *(Matching)*

Activities for Karen, Jack and Olivia

The following texts offer information about different holiday activities.

- *Decide which of the holiday activities in the texts (A–E) is the most suitable for the teenagers below (1–3).*
- *Write the correct letters in the box next to the picture.*

Tipp

Vorsicht!
Hier geht es um drei Menschen, aber sechs Aktivitäten (A–E). Du darfst jede Aktivität nur einem Menschen zuschreiben. Drei von den Sätzen (A–E) werden also ungenutzt bleiben.

1	[E]	Karen loves discovering and exploring new places. Her financial resources are limited, so she is prepared to put up with fairly basic accommodation. She is more interested in spending time with like-minded people, as eager as she is to tackle new experiences and challenges.
2	[D]	Jack is a sports freak, and does well in everything from football to climbing, from kayaking to camping. He does well in both team and individual sports. But while he loves doing sport himself, his passion during the holidays is to share these skills with children from deprived areas of the country.
3	[C]	Olivia is into arts and crafts of all kinds. She makes her own clothes, she restores and paints old furniture, and she has even done a course in colouring glass. Rather than doing more of a skill in which she is already well versed, however, she prefers new challenges to test herself against.

A
The Buxton Sports Academy offers holiday courses in a range of sports that include sailing, tennis, climbing, boxing and squash, as well as team sports such as football, rugby and hockey. Professional coaches who are used to working with young people give a thorough training and develop each individual's skills.

Tipp

Jack mag Sport – und doch ist **A** nicht die richtige Antwort. Er sucht etwas anderes. Siehst du was?

_____

B
Many families have old chairs or faded chests of drawers up in the attic or out in the garden shed – pieces of furniture that were once a source of pride and joy, and which could become so again. This 5-day residential course teaches students how to remove old paint and varnish, how to deal with stains and woodworm, and how to bring colour back into faded wood. Suitable for beginners or experienced wood workers.

Tipp

Furniture kommt bei Olivia vor – und doch ist **B** nicht die richtige Antwort. Warum nicht?

_____

C

The Haxby Pottery Farm runs residential pottery courses for all ages and abilities. Create your own pots or sculptures, and make vases for your home or ceramic presents to give away. It's a great way to develop your pottery skills or learn a new craft, and make new friends. Phone Edna on 01826 34591 for more details.

E

Three intrepid hikers are looking for a fourth member to join them on a ten-day hike in the Italian Alps. Overnight stays in mountain huts and shelters, or in tents if necessary. We have an old car to get us to Italy and ask for a contribution towards the cost of the fuel.

D

Every year we run a 2-week residential camp in the heart of the Derbyshire Dales for inner-city children from the Greater Manchester area. The children have been selected by social workers working with families in some of the poorest inner-city wards, with the aim of giving the children new opportunities and their parents a break. We always need volunteer assistants to help us run the courses: we cover board and lodging, but can offer no pay.

Richtig/Falsch-Aufgaben mit Zeilenangaben *(True/False with line reference)*

Kasun

The following text is a dialogue between Kasun and Sahan, boys in Sri Lanka, at Kasun's first day at school.

- *Read the text. Then look at the statements.*
- *For each statement tick (✓) the correct answer 'true' or 'false' and give the line(s) in which you find the information.*

"Hey, what's your name?"
I turned round and saw a big boy. He was smiling. But was he talking to me? Or to somebody behind me? I didn't dare answer.
5 "Hey, what's the problem?" said the boy, and took a step closer to me. I couldn't help but see his big hands. Was he going to hit me?
"Do you think I'm going to bite you?" He laughed.
"Hi. I'm Sahan."
10 "I ... I'm Kasun," I stuttered. "I'm not from Colombo. I'm from Kuruwita, but I ..."
"Hey, calm down, you're talking too fast," laughed Sahan.

Tipp

Manchmal musst du aus dem Text schließen, was passiert ist oder wie ein Mensch sich fühlt.

Satz 2: *scared* steht nicht im Text, nicht mal das Synonym *frightened*. Wie weißt du aber, dass Kasun Angst hat?

___

Satz 3: *nervous* steht nicht im Text. Woher weißt du dann, dass Kasun aufgeregt ist?

___

		true	false	line(s)
1	Kasun doesn't answer the boy's first question because he was so big.	☐	☒	2–3
2	When the boy comes nearer to him, Kasun is scared.	☒	☐	6–7
3	Kasun's reaction suggests that he is very nervous.	☒	☐	10–11

TRAINING SECTION: Reading

3. Leseverstehen – *Now you*

In diesem Kapitel kannst du die Strategien, die du auf den letzten Seiten kennen gelernt hast, mit ausgewählten Aufgaben zum Leseverstehen gezielt üben. Grundlage dafür sind Werbeanzeigen für unterschiedliche Veranstaltungen, eine Auswahl an Stellenanzeigen für Praktika, ein Artikel über die Filmindustrie in Neuseeland sowie ein Blog über ein Motorrad-Rennen auf der Isle of Man.

Part 1 – Richtig/Falsch-Aufgaben *(True/False)*

What's on?

- *Read the texts below. Then read the statements (1–5).*
- *Decide whether the statements are true or false.*
- *Then tick (✓) the correct box.*

What's on

Karen Pahlavi worked for three years in South America, and took amazing photos at archaeological sites such as Machu Picchu. Her stunning photographs are now on show in the City Library. The exhibition runs until the end of November.

10 am to 5 pm

Pay what you think.

Tickets to watch the England v Pakistan cricket match next May are now on sale.

This sure-to-be-exciting game will be an important part of England's preparation as they seek to win the *Test Series* later in the year.

Tickets: Adult £45-£65, U16 £15-£25

Order your tickets online. Don't miss out: we predict that this event will be sold out by the end of November.

Lead up to a sparkling Christmas as you skate on real ice at the annual outdoor skating rink in the yard opposite the Castle.

And every Wednesday and Sunday evenings our rink becomes the coolest dancing floor in town during special disco sessions.

All our prices include skate hire. Book online and get over 10% off.

Rich Pickings at the Polo Theatre

One actor. One hour. One of the funniest shows you'll ever see. Barbara Newman is incredible in this solo role, in which she investigates the life of investors, bankers and accountants in the City of London. Hilarious, passionate, hard-hitting – this is a show you'll never forget.

7.30 pm from Monday to Saturday, 2 pm matinee on Saturday, 26 November. £12.

		true	false
1	The skating rink is an indoor event.		✗
2	*Rich Pickings* is a play that makes the audience laugh.	✗	
3	The match is part of the *Test Series* competition.		✗
4	There are tickets still available for the cricket match – but probably not for long.	✗	
5	You can choose how much money you want to give when you visit the photo exhibition at the Library.	✗	

TRAINING SECTION: Reading

Part 2 – Zuordnungsaufgaben *(Matching)*

Work practice assignments

> - Decide which of the work practice assignments described in the texts (A–H) is the most suitable for the teenagers below (1–5).
> - Write the correct letter in the box next to the picture.

1		Jonny has always been interested in things that grow. One of his favourite possessions is the microscope that his parents gave him for his last birthday because he loves analysing what leaves and flowers look like when magnified. But he's even happier when he can follow up his interest outdoors.
2		Samina started making things when she was only three years old. She began by sticking things together, then she went through a phase of knitting, and now she loves working creatively with wood, making both stand-alone works of art and practical objects for around the house.
3		Tadek speaks fluent Polish, German and English, but as though that is not enough he is also teaching himself Arabic and Japanese. "Languages are the key to meeting people," he says, "and there's nothing more fascinating in the world than people."
4		Katja loves making cakes, brownies and biscuits, and likes trying to make different sorts of bread. Not surprising that her favourite TV show is the Great British Bake-Off! Her most recent discovery is a sweet loaf traditionally made at Easter in the Ukraine.
5		Zoe is a friendly, tolerant person, but what makes her really angry is poor website design. She can't stand sites that look boring, are difficult to use or have information that is out of date. "There's no excuse for it," she says. "It's easy enough to produce an attractive web design – even quite a complicated one."

A

We welcome students to our friendly chemist's shop just off the market square. You will help serve customers and will have the opportunity to help us decorate the shop in the all-important lead-up to Christmas. In addition to medicines and cosmetics we also serve lunchtime sandwiches.

B

Tourists come to our city from all over the world, and many want to know more about our city's fascinating history. Here at *City Tours* we provide walking tours in an ever-growing number of different languages. Do your work experience here and you are sure to engage with interested clients from around the globe.

C

Horace's is the largest Garden Centre in town, with the widest choice of trees, shrubs and plants. We are happy to train students who share our passion for everything that grows in the garden. In addition to working at the till, you will learn how to breed plants from seeds and how to pack plants safely for orders by post.

D

K&J Logistics (formerly *Liptons Removals*) have been in the business of moving homes for over 100 years and enjoy an enviable reputation for reliability. We deal both with moves within our city and moves to countries abroad, and we have recently developed a new line in renting out vans. Your work experience will of course involve some carrying of furniture, but we'll also give you useful advice on looking after engines.

E

This is a young and innovative company, and in your work experience here you'll find yourself working with people not much older than yourself! Some will be working on new computer games, others will be developing apps for customers as varied as *United Biscuits* and *Featherstone Tyres*. What unites us is a passion for good quality digital work – and if you have good ideas in this field, we'll be happy to hear them!

F

Little People provides a safe, happy environment for pre-school children. We open at 7 am each workday and can look after your child for an hour or two, or all the way through till we close at 6 pm. All our assistants are qualified and of course we provide all children with snacks and meals.

G

I taught Technology for several years before setting up a new business as a freelance carpenter. My first orders were for chairs and window frames, but I have been able to branch out and tackle orders like shepherd's huts and church pews. I now have two full-time assistants, so in your work experience you will be in a team of four. I'll show you how to use a wide range of tools and help you to practise a range of skills. Welcome to the team!

H

We opened our shop three years ago, when Karen spotted the lack of a baker's shop in this part of town. Since then we have grown from success to success, with our fresh bakery products flying off the shelves. Come and join us for your work experience, and you'll pick up baking tips and tricks that will be useful to you for life.

Part 3 – Auswahlaufgaben *(Multiple choice)*

- *Read the text and tick (✓) the correct statement.*
- *There is only one correct solution per statement.*

Filming in New Zealand

This text is taken from an article in a film magazine.

New Zealand's breathtaking landscape has long attracted the world's top film directors.

The *Lord of the Rings* trilogy, for example, was filmed in different areas of New Zealand, mainly, though not exclusively, in the country's national parks. The films made use of spectacular mountains such as Mount Ngauruhoe, a treeless live volcano, and of rivers, lakes and wild canyons. But scenes were also filmed in the softer and less dramatic looking green hills near Matamata. One of the advantages of filming in New Zealand is that the population density is so low, with only four and half million people in a country more or less the same size as the United Kingdom (population 64 million). So there are fewer buildings, roads and power lines to spoil the views of open countryside.

However, New Zealand's cities have also featured in films. In the film *King Kong*, for example, many of the scenes supposedly set in New York were actually filmed in Wellington, New Zealand's capital, though not its largest city. This means that the southernmost capital city in the world has a thriving film industry, and professional experience of working with some leading film directors.

The Lord of the Rings – The Fellowship of the Ring (USA/NZ 2001)

1 The *Lord of the Rings* trilogy was filmed …

a) ☐ in various regions of New Zealand.
b) ☐ in national parks only.
c) ☐ in just one part of New Zealand.
d) ☐ on Mt Ngauruhoe only.

2 All the scenes of the film were filmed …

a) ☐ in wild hills near Matamata.
b) ☐ in spectacular and less spectacular scenery.
c) ☐ on a volcano famous for its trees.
d) ☐ in the most dramatic parts of the country.

3 New Zealand has …

a) ☐ fewer people per square kilometre than the United Kingdom.
b) ☐ about as many people per square kilometre as the United Kingdom.
c) ☐ more people per square kilometre than the United Kingdom.
d) ☐ about the same number of inhabitants as the United Kingdom.

4 Wellington …

a) ☐ is New Zealand's biggest city.
b) ☐ is too far south to be the capital city.
c) ☐ has good scenery but no local film industry.
d) ☐ is further south than any other capital city.

TRAINING SECTION: Reading

Part 4 – Richtig/Falsch-Aufgaben mit Zeilenangaben *(True/False with line reference)*

- *Read the text, then look at the statements.*
- *For each statement tick (✓) the correct answer true or false and give the line(s) in which you find the information.*
- *For a correct answer you must fill in both: true or false and the line(s).*

The Isle of Man TT race

The Isle of Man is a small island between Britain and Ireland. It is famous for its motorcycle racing. This text is from a blog written by a resident on the Isle of Man.

I live on one of Europe's quietest islands – the Isle of Man, set in the Irish Sea about halfway between England and Ireland. We have beautiful unspoilt countryside, narrow country
5 roads, and every May or June we have the TT (Tourist Trophy) race. It's one of the most famous motorcycle racing events in the world, and the amazing thing is that it takes place on about 50 kilometres of our narrow public lanes.

10 Every year, the roads are closed to the public for a week of practice runs followed by a week of racing. That means a fortnight of road chaos on the island, when it's hard for locals to get from one part of the island to another.

15 The only way you can bring your motorbike is by ferry, and in 2015 about 36,000 fans travelled to the Isle of Man, bringing more than 14,000 motorbikes with them – an increase of 17 % compared to the year before.

20 The TT has run every year since 1907, with the exception of the years during the First and Second World Wars. It has not always been popular with racers, however. Between 1907 and 2015 no less than 246 people have lost their
25 lives during the event – 141 competitors, and 105 spectators and other members of the public.

Tourist Trophy race, Isle of Man (2015)

As a result, the event was boycotted by a number of leading motorbike riders and sponsors in the early 1970s.

The event is a huge boost to the island's 30
economy, but not everybody is in favour of it. I, for one, am not a motorbike fan, and I hate the crowds and the noise. But I have learned to deal with it: I just book my holidays while the racing takes place. That way, I avoid the bustle while 35
I sunbathe on a beach in Turkey or Spain, and I pay for my holiday by letting my little house to TT visitors.

		true	false	line(s)
1	In the TT event the motorbikes race on a specially made track.	☐	☐	_____
2	The roads are closed for two weeks for the Isle of Man TT race.	☐	☐	_____
3	The number of bikes brought to the Isle of Man in 2015 was higher than 2014.	☐	☐	_____
4	In the early 1970s there were no TT races.	☐	☐	_____
5	The writer only sees disadvantages in the TT event.	☐	☐	_____

Sprachmittlung – *Mediating*

1. Ablauf und Bewertung der Prüfung

Die Prüfung

Die geschriebene Prüfung besteht aus **Hörverstehen, Leseverstehen, Mediating** und **Schreiben**. Für das Ganze hast du 120 Minuten Zeit. Zusätzlich erhältst du 15 Minuten Auswahlzeit, in der du dich für ein Writing Set entscheiden kannst.

Ablauf beim Mediating

Bei der Sprachmittlung vermittelst du zwischen einem deutsch- und einem englischsprachigen Sprecher. Du sollst nicht Wort für Wort übersetzen, sondern das Wichtige in deinen Worten übertragen. Danach liest du einen deutschen (oder englischen) Text und erzählst die wichtigsten Punkte auf Englisch (oder Deutsch).

Bewertung beim Mediating

Ein zweisprachiges oder elektronisches Wörterbuch ist erlaubt.
Du brauchst keine Angst vor Grammatik- oder Rechtschreibfehlern in deinen Antworten zu haben. Solange man versteht, was du geschrieben hast, gehen sie in diesem Prüfungsteil nicht in die Bewertung ein. Beim Mediating wird jede Lösung akzeptiert, durch die der Empfänger die Mitteilung versteht und darauf angemessen reagieren kann.

Verbringe nicht zu viel Zeit mit Mediating: Dieser Prüfungsteil macht nur ungefähr 10 % der schriftlichen Prüfung (6 % der Gesamtnote) aus.

2. Typische Aufgabenformate in Niedersachsen

In diesem Kapitel lernst du die typischen Aufgabenformate kennen, die dich bei der Abschlussprüfung im Bereich Mediating erwarten. Die blauen Tipp-Kästen enthalten nützliche Strategien, wie du mit häufigen Schwierigkeiten umgehen kannst.

1 Die Ausgangssituation

Eine Situation wird beschrieben, in der eine deutschsprachige Person mit einer englischsprachigen Person kommunizieren muss. Sie verstehen sich nicht.
Du aber sprichst beide Sprachen – also kannst du sprachmitteln.

> *You want to join the football club in town and go for an interview with the club coach. In front of you in the queue is Adelola, a girl from Nigeria. Adelola doesn't speak German, and the coach doesn't speak English.*
>
> *So you help Adelola and the coach to communicate.*

Tipp

Der Rahmen kann auf Englisch oder auf Deutsch gegeben werden.
Es geht immer darum, dass du zwischen zwei Parteien vermitteln sollst.

– Wer spricht hier Englisch?
  _____

– Wer spricht hier Deutsch?
  _____

TRAINING SECTION: Mediating

2 Mediating von gesprochenen Sätzen

Du sollst die Worte der deutschsprachigen Person sinngemäß auf Englisch wiedergeben, und umgekehrt. Es handelt sich meistens um drei bis vier Aussagen.

Adelola In Nigeria I played in a team with boys and girls. Are there mixed teams in this club? Or do boys and girls compete in different teams?

You (1) _____

Coach Wir hatten bisher immer getrennte Mannschaften für Jungen und andere für Mädchen.

You (2) _____

Coach Wir haben aber Pläne für gemischte Mannschaften. Wir denken da an ein neues Turnier mit gemischten Mannschaften nächstes Jahr. Ich hole mal eine Broschüre dazu.

You (3) _____

> **Tipp**
> Beim Mediating sollst du nur das Wichtigste übertragen. Was ist das hier:
> a) Adelolas Aussage über Nigeria und die zwei Fragen?
> b) Beide Fragen?
> c) Nur eine von den beiden Fragen?

> **Tipp**
> Markiere die Teile der Aussage, die du übertragen sollst.

> **Tipp**
> Markiere wieder die Teile der Aussage, die du übertragen sollst.
> Die Zahlen in Klammern sind keine Punkteangaben. Es sind Aufgaben 1, 2 und 3.

3 Mediating von einem Text

Nun sollst du einen Text auf Deutsch lesen, in dem es um dasselbe Thema wie im Dialog geht. Die englischsprachige Person aus dem Dialog stellt ein paar Fragen zum Text, und du sollst die Informationen auf Englisch wiedergeben. Außerdem sollst du Informationen aussuchen, die für die andere Person von Interesse sein könnten.

> *While the coach is getting a leaflet from his office, Adelola says that she would really like to take part in the mixed teams competition.*
> *She would like to know when the first mixed teams will play, whether she is old enough to play (she is 16 now), and how teams qualify as mixed teams. Answer Adelola's questions (4–6) and give two more pieces of information that you think are relevant for her (7–8) from the leaflet below.*

> **Tipp**
> Der einleitende Text ist kompakt. Notiere, was du machen musst:
> 1 Wie viele Fragen musst du beantworten: 3, 4 oder 6?
> _____
> 2 Markiere die Fragen im Text.
> 3 Musst du sonst etwas machen?
> _____

(4) _____

(5) _____

(6) _____

Your additional pieces of information for Adelola:

(7) _____

(8) _____

Neues Turnier mit gemischten Mannschaften

Die Fußballklubs unserer Region haben eine lange Tradition, fürchten sich aber nicht vor neuen Entwicklungen. Dazu gehört die Erfahrung in immer mehr Sportvereinen, dass Jungen und Mädchen davon profitieren, wenn sie die Gelegenheit haben, nach Altersklassen zusammen zu trainieren und zu spielen.

Aus diesem Grunde hat sich die Stadt für ein Turnier mit gemischten Jungen- und Mädchen-Mannschaften entschieden. Es werden im ersten Jahr drei Altersgruppen zugelassen:

– Gruppe A: Mannschaften von 11- und 12-jährigen,
– Gruppe B: Mannschaften von 13- und 14-jährigen,
– Gruppe C: Mannschaften von 15- und 16-jährigen.

Die Spiele der ersten Runde des Turniers finden im September nächsten Jahres statt. Meldeschluss für die Mannschaften ist Ende Mai. Die nähere Organisation des Turniers ist davon abhängig, wie viele Mannschaften sich für das Turnier melden. Details dazu wird es bis Ende Juli geben. Wir hoffen, dass ältere Spieler sowohl beim Training der Jüngeren als auch bei der Organisation des Turniers helfen werden.

Nach ersten Kontakten mit den Fußballklubs in unserer Region rechnet die Stadt mit einem großen Zulauf an Interessenten. Das gilt sowohl für Teilnehmer als auch für Zuschauer. Es ist unsere Hoffnung, dass das neue Turnier zu einer jährlichen Institution wird, und dass der Rahmen sich über die nächsten Jahre erweitert, sodass auch ältere Spieler und Spielerinnen zukünftig teilnehmen können.

Mannschaften werden nur dann zugelassen, wenn sie aus mindestens vier Jungen und mindestens vier Mädchen bestehen.

Die Teilnahmegebühr beträgt € 20,00 pro Mannschaft. Es wird für dieses erste Turnier spezielle T-Shirts und Erinnerungsmedaillen geben.

Tipp

Um zu entscheiden, was Adelola interessieren könnte:
Versuche die Sache mit **ihren** Augen zu sehen und frag dich, was du über sie weißt.

Du hast z. B. erfahren, dass sie gerne in so einem Turnier spielen möchte – gibt es da Chancen?

TRAINING SECTION: Mediating

4 Mediating mit Pronomenwechsel

Sumon, a boy from Bangladesh, is new in your class. One evening, you and your German friend Axel invite Sumo to go swimming with you. On the way home from the pool, Axel stops at a fast food stand. Axel doesn't speak English as well as you, so he asks you to mediate.

Axel He, das riecht gut! Und ich weiß, an diesem Stand kriegt man besonders gute vegetarische Currywurst. Ich hätte Lust auf eine, du auch? Und ich kaufe auch Sumon eine. Die Currywurstsoße wird ihm schmecken, das garantiere ich.

You (1) _____

Sumon Hey, that's really kind of him. Do please thank him. I wonder if the sauce is a bit like our Bangladeshi sauces?

You (2) _____

Sumon Mmm, I really like the sausage. But the sauce is a bit strange, not what I was expecting. It isn't like an Asian sauce at all.

You (3) _____

> **Tipp**
>
> Vorsicht beim Perspektivwechsel!
> Axel sagt: **Ich** hätte Lust auf ...
> Du sagst: **Axel** wants to ...
>
> Sumon sagt: **I** wonder if ...
> Du sagst: _____ gespannt, ob ...
>
> Sumon sagt: **I** really like the sausage.
> Du sagst: _____

> **Tipp**
>
> Manche „typisch deutsche" Alltagsdinge oder Traditionen kennt dein Gegenüber eventuell nicht. Hierfür gibt es im Englischen meist gar keinen direkten Begriff. Du musst dann erklären, was du meinst.
> Typische Beispiele sind neben der Currywurst Dinge wie Rosenmontag, Schultüte, Brezel, Weihnachtsmarkt, ...

The next day, you find information online about the origins of curry in Europe.
Sumon is interested, and wants to know when curry first came to Europe, why the curry in Europe tastes different to curry in Asia, and when the *Currywurst* was invented?

Look at the text below. Answer Sumon's questions (4–6) and give two more pieces of information that you think will interest him (7–8).

(4) _____

(5) _____

(6) _____

Your additional pieces of information for Sumon:

(7) _____

(8) _____

Tatsächlich ist die Geschichte von Curry in Europa mit militärischer Geschichte verstrickt.

Im 19. Jahrhundert eroberte und besetzte Großbritannien weite Strecken von Asien. Tausende von britischen Beamten, Ingenieuren und Soldaten wohnten in Asien und das Essen, das sie dort bekamen, schmeckte ihnen sehr. Sie nannten es *curry*.

Zurück in Großbritannien wollten diese Leute ihr *curry* weiter genießen. Es war aber wegen des langen Seewegs äußerst schwierig, die notwendigen frischen Kräuter und Gewürze in Europa zu finden. Stattdessen verwendeten die britischen Köche und Köchinnen eine eintönige Mischung aus getrockneten Kräutern und Gewürzen – ein gelbes Puver, das sie *curry powder* nannten und zu einer Soße machten. Die unendlich vielen und variierten Rezepte aus Asien wurden also durch dieses eine Standardessen ersetzt.

In Asien selber kann man *curry* nicht mal kaufen. Es wäre so absurd, wie nach einer Suppe zu fragen, ohne die Art zu nennen.

Früh im 20. Jahrhundert wanderten immer mehr Menschen aus Asien nach Großbritannien ein. Sie stammten hauptsächlich aus Bangladesch und Pakistan. Man nannte sie aber *Indians*, da Bangladesch und Pakistan damals zum britischen Reich *India* gehörten. Als manche von ihnen Restaurants eröffneten, nannte man diese auch *Indian restaurants*. Das ist übrigens in

Großbritannien immer noch der Fall, obwohl die Inhaber von weit über der Hälfte aller *'Indian' restaurants* eigentlich aus Bangladesch kommen.

Auch die deutsche Currywurst hat mit militärischer Geschichte zu tun, nämlich mit der Besetzung Norddeutschlands durch britische Truppen nach dem Ende des Zweiten Weltkriegs. Denn die britischen Soldaten brachten zwei in Großbritannien gut bekannte Soßen mit: *ketchup* und *Worcester Sauce*. In Deutschland hatte man die Idee, diese Soßen zu kombinieren, und die so entstandene Soße mit Bratwurst zu essen – das war die Geburt der Currywurst.

Umstritten ist, ob die allererste Wurst in Berlin, in Hamburg oder im Ruhrgebiet erfunden wurde. Unumstritten ist aber die Tatsache, dass in allen drei Gebieten tausende von britischen Soldaten wohnten.

Schreiben – *Writing*

1. Ablauf und Bewertung der Prüfung

Die Prüfung

Die geschriebene Prüfung besteht aus **Hörverstehen, Leseverstehen, Mediating** und **Schreiben**. Für das Ganze hast du 120 Minuten Zeit.

Ablauf beim Writing

Dieser Teil der Prüfung besteht aus zwei Writing Sets, z. B.
– zwei kurze Texte von je 50 Wörtern und einen längeren Text von 120 Wörtern,
– einen mittleren Text von 80 Wörtern und einen längeren Text von 120 Wörtern.
Du erhältst fünfzehn Minuten Auswahlzeit, in der du dich für ein Writing Set entscheiden kannst.
Ein zweisprachiges oder ein elektronisches Wörterbuch ist erlaubt.

Bewertung beim Writing

Das Schreiben macht etwa 19 % deiner Gesamtnote aus.
Die Punkte beim Schreiben werden für **Inhalt** und **Sprache** vergeben. Du kannst 25 Punkte erreichen.
Folgende Kriterien tragen zu deiner Note bei:

- **Inhalt:** Es gibt Punkte dafür, dass du …
    - die Aufgabe vollständig löst,
    - alle Aspekte eindeutig, detailliert und differenziert darstellst,
    - nur wenige Wiederholungen und Abschweifungen hast,
    - deinen Text kohärent (= zusammenhängend) und logisch gliederst.

- **Sprache:** Es gibt Punkte dafür, dass …
    - das Lesen deines Textes keine Mühe bereitet,
    - es sich um einen sehr klar formulierten Text handelt,
    - du komplexe Sätze bildest (mit Haupt- und Nebensätzen, *time phrases* etc.)
    - dein Text durch Verwendung von Bindewörtern (Konnektoren) logisch aufgebaut ist,
    - du einen vielseitigen und zutreffenden Wortschatz und idiomatische Wendungen benutzt,
    - du die Wörter richtig schreibst,
    - du verschiedene grammatische Strukturen sicher verwendest,
    - man versteht, was du sagen willst, auch wenn bei komplizierten Sätzen vereinzelte Wortschatz- oder Grammatikfehler vorkommen.

2. Typische Aufgabenformate in Niedersachsen

Im Folgenden lernst du beispielhafte Aufgabenformate kennen, die dich bei der Abschlussprüfung im Bereich Schreiben erwarten können.
Die blauen Kästen enthalten nützliche Hinweise und Hilfen.

TRAINING SECTION: Writing

The 50 word text

1 Die Arbeitsanweisungen

Lies die Arbeitsanweisungen.

Tipp
Markiere in den Anweisungsangaben, worüber du schreiben sollst.

> Your English exchange partner is doing a project about towns and young people, and has asked you to write something about your town or village.
> - Give some general information about your town/village.
> - Say what life is like there for young people.
> - Say what you like best about your town/village.
>
> Write about 50 words. Count your words.

2 Wie wird dein Text bewertet?

Du kannst fünf Punkte erreichen, wenn dein **Inhalt** und deine **Sprache** angemessen und überzeugend sind und du deinen Text so eindeutig formulierst, dass eventuelle Fehler die Verständlichkeit nicht beeinträchtigen. Gar keinen Punkt gibt es, wenn du das Thema verfehlst und die Ausführungen unverständlich sind.

Oxford

3 Inhalt

Wie kannst du dir am besten **Inhaltspunkte** sichern? **Sammle Ideen** und **mache einen kurzen Plan**.

Mache Notizen:
— Was ist in deiner Stadt gut für junge Leute?
— Was ist schwierig?

Tipp
Nicht alle Schüler machen Notizen auf dieselbe Weise. Und in der Prüfung hast du nicht viel Zeit. Finde also heraus, was **dir** am besten hilft:
— **Einzelwörter auf Englisch?**
— **Einzelwörter auf Deutsch?**
— **ein Netzwerk** oder **Mindmap**?
— **zwei Listen**?
— **oder etwas anderes**?
Hier gibt es keine allgemeingültige Antwort. Es gibt nur die Antwort, die aus deiner Erfahrung für **dich** zutrifft.

4 Sprache

Gewöhne dich daran, deinen fertigen Text noch einmal gut durchzulesen und auf Fehler zu prüfen.

a) Lies dieses Beispiel.
Achtung: Die blau markierten Wörter sind fehlerhaft.
Lies die Informationen in den Kästen und verbessere die Fehler.

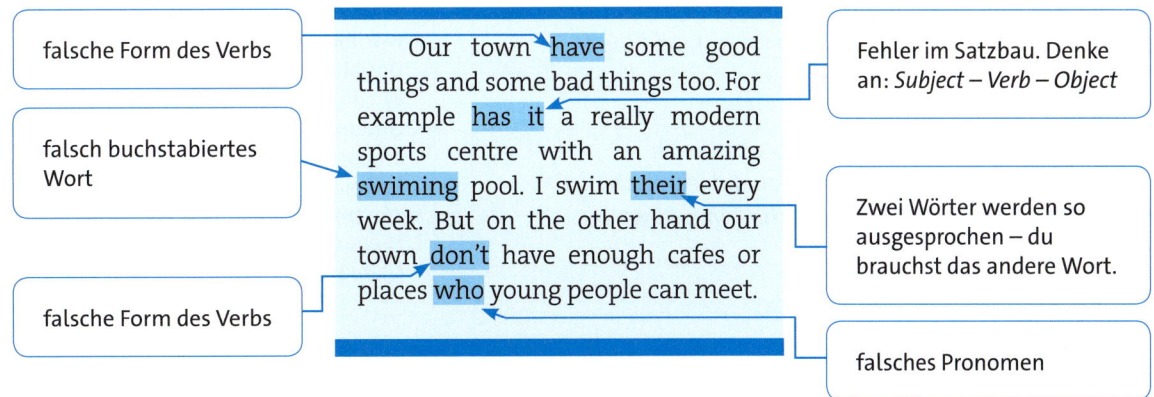

TRAINING SECTION: Writing

b) Now write your text.

> - Give some general information about your town/village.
> - Say what life is like there for young people:
>   - What's good in your town for young people?
>   - What's not so good?
> - Say what you like best about your town/village.

Tipp

Schreibe nun deinen eigenen Text.
Verwende den Plan, den du in Abschnitt 3 gemacht hast.

c) Überprüfe deinen Text auf mögliche Fehler.
– Stimmen die Verben und die Zeiten?
– Stimmt der Satzbau?
– Sind alle Wörter richtig geschrieben?
– Hast du an einer Stelle eventuell das falsche Wort verwendet?
– ...?

5 Jetzt bist du Prüferin oder Prüfer ☺!

Schau dir noch einmal die Bewertungskriterien in Abschnitt 2 an. Dann lies deinen Text erneut durch und entscheide, wie viele Punkte er verdient.
Falls möglich, wäre es noch besser, wenn du deinen Text mit jemandem tauschen kannst. Lies den anderen Text und entscheide, wie viele Punkte er bekommen sollte.

The 80 word text

1 Die Arbeitsanweisungen

Sieh dir die Bilder an und lies die Arbeitsanweisungen.

> The three pictures are from a trip that you did last weekend. Write about your trip for a short blog to accompany the photos.
> Include:
> - where you went and who you went with
> - a short description of what you did (three things)
> - whether or not you enjoyed the trip and why.
> Write about 80 words.

Tipp

Markiere in den Anweisungsangaben, worüber du schreiben sollst.
Das allerletzte Wort *why* ist auch das Wichtigste. Bei Texten mit diesem Umfang wird erwartet, dass du **Gründe** angibst und deine **Meinung** äußerst, zum Beispiel:
The trip was great because ...
I enjoyed the trip although ...
I didn't enjoy the trip at all because ...

TRAINING SECTION: Writing

2 Wie wird dein Text bewertet?

Du kannst zehn Punkte erreichen. Geachtet wird wieder auf **Inhalt und Sprache**.
Du bekommst die volle Punktzahl, wenn dein Text sehr kohärent und detailreich ist und du die Aufgabe ausführlich, strukturiert und klar gelöst hast. Für eine gelungene Arbeit verwendest du einen abwechslungsreichen Wortschatz, einen variablen Satzbau und machst nur wenige Fehler.

Schlecht bewertet wird dein Text hingegen, wenn du die Aufgabe nur ansatzweise löst, kein oder nur wenig innerer Zusammenhang in deinem Text erkennbar ist und wenn zahlreiche sprachliche Verstöße den Text schwer verständlich machen.

3 Inhalt und Sprache

Hier ist ein Beispieltext.

a) Inhalt
Markiere die Stellen, die den Inhalt der Aufgabe erfüllen:
   – *where you went*
   – *who you went with*
   – *what you did (three things)*
   – *whether or not you enjoyed the trip*
   – *why*

b) Satzbau
Nebensätze gehen über einfache Satzmuster hinaus. Markiere die Nebensätze.

c) Grammatik
Unterstreiche
   – die negative Form von zwei Verben,
   – zwei Verben im *past perfect*,
   – ein Adjektiv im Superlativ.

d) Wortschatz
Notiere hier:
   – Verben im *simple past*: _weren't, didn't, was, were, had, went_
   – Adjektive: _____
   – *linking words* (Konnektoren): _because, but, when_

> Last weekend I went with my friend Sam on a camping trip in the mountains. Dave had wanted to come too, but he didn't have time because he had so much homework. We hiked along muddy valleys, we climbed steep hills and in the evening we cooked on an open fire. Although the weather was awful, it was great fun. The wet nights weren't great, but it was a great feeling when I stood on the highest mountain that I had ever climbed!

4 Jetzt bist du Prüferin oder Prüfer ☺!

Schau dir noch einmal die Bewertungskriterien in Abschnitt 2 an.
Dann lies den Text in 3 erneut durch und entscheide,
wie viele Punkte der Text verdient und warum.

Punkte: _____

Begründung: _____

37

TRAINING SECTION: Writing

The 120 word text: Making an argument

1 Die Arbeitsanweisungen

Lies die Arbeitsanweisungen.

> *You are spending a year at a school in England, where the students are discussing the pros and cons of weekend jobs. You are asked to write an article for the school magazine about this topic and your experience of weekend jobs in Germany.*
> *Include*
> - *some basic information about weekend jobs in Germany*
> - *advantages and disadvantages of weekend jobs*
> - *your opinion (give reasons).*
> *Write an article of about 120 words.*

2 Mache dir Notizen zu den drei Punkten in der Aufgabenstellung.

Getting a weekend job is a stupid idea while you are still at school.

— basic information about weekend jobs in Germany: _____

— advantages of weekend jobs: *become independent, ...*

— disadvantages of weekend jobs: *less time for homework, ...*

— my opinion (with reasons): _____

3 Wie werden Inhalt und Sprache bei längeren Schreibaufgaben bewertet?

Für diese Aufgabe kannst du 15 Punkte bekommen: 7,5 Punkte für den Inhalt und 7,5 Punkte für die Sprache. Um die volle Punktzahl zu erhalten, musst du **inhaltlich** die Aufgabe vollständig gelöst haben. Deine Argumente und der Handlungsverlauf sind schlüssig. Es gibt keine unklaren Stellen und der Text ist zusammenhängend. **Sprachlich** hast du deinen Text logisch aufgebaut, sodass das Lesen keine Mühe bereitet. Du benutzt einen breiten Wortschatz und zeigst eine gute Verwendung von Konnektoren. Außerdem bist du sicher in den grammatischen Strukturen und machst nur vereinzelte Fehler.

4 Nun schreibe deinen Text.

- Beginne mit einer kurzen Einleitung, die klarmacht, worum es hier geht.
- Führe Argumente für und gegen das Statement auf und belege sie mit Beispielen.
- Gib deine eigene Meinung.
- Achte auf deine Sprache.

5 Überprüfe deinen Text.

Hake die aufgelisteten Punkte in der Checkliste ab.

a) Die Aufgabenstellung ist erfüllt, denn mein Text enthält ...

some basic information about weekend jobs in Germany	☐
advantages and disadvantages of weekend jobs	☐
my opinion (with reasons)	☐

b) Das Lesen bereitet keine Mühe, denn mein Text zeichnet sich aus durch ...

einen logischen Aufbau	☐
einen breiten Wortschatz	☐
die gute Verwendung von *linking words (and, but, so, because, on the one hand, ...)*	☐
die sichere Verwendung der Grammatik	☐
wenige Fehler	☐

6 Jetzt bist du Prüferin oder Prüfer ☺!

Schau dir noch einmal die Bewertungskriterien in Abschnitt 3 an.
Entscheide, wie viele Punkte dein Text verdient und warum.

Punkte: _____

Begründung: _____

The 120 word text: Creative writing

1 Die Arbeitsanweisungen

Lies die Arbeitsanweisungen.

> *Write a story for an online competition.*
>
> *The topic is: What a surprise!*
> *Here are some ideas.*
> *You could write a story about*
> - *a meeting,*
> - *an event,*
> - *a message.*
>
> *Write your own story in about 120 words.*
> *Your story must*
> - *have a relevant title,*
> - *be interesting to read,*
> - *have a logical plot related to a surprise.*

Tipp
Notiere Ideen zu allen Punkten, die in der Arbeitsanweisung erwähnt sind.

2 Mache dir zunächst Notizen.

Mache dir Notizen zum Inhalt deiner Erzählung.
– Title   – How the story started   – What happened then   – What was the big surprise?

3 Sprache

Lies nun dieses Beispiel für einen gelungenen Text.
Warum werden die markierten Stellen von der **Sprache** her besonders viele Punkte bringen?
Ordne die Kriterien A–F den Textstellen zu. Die Kriterien können mehrmals vorkommen.

Wortschatz	Grammatik	Satzstruktur
A breiter Wortschatz	**B** Vielfalt an grammatischen Strukturen	**C** unterschiedliche Satzanfänge **D** in den Text integrierter Dialog **E** Fragesätze **F** Nebensätze

TRAINING SECTION: Writing

B: Vielfalt an grammatischen Strukturen

An unexpected meeting

Dave had never wanted to work in a clothes shop, but he was happy when he got a job in the clothes shop next to his school. Still, on his first day at work he was very nervous. Would he make some stupid mistakes? Would the other workers be nice to him?

Everything started well, but then suddenly Dave dropped a box full of new shirts onto the floor. He went on his hands and knees to pick them up – and this is how he was when the door opened and a customer came in.

Dave looked up to say sorry, and that's when he had his enormous surprise. The customer was Max Kingdom, Dave's favourite film star. "Well, good morning," said Max, "have you lost something?"

3 Schreibe jetzt deine Geschichte.

Denke an einen logischen und klaren Aufbau und verwende Nebensätze, Fragesätze, unterschiedliche Satzanfänge und eine Vielfalt an grammatischen Strukturen.

4 Überprüfe deinen Text auf …

a) **Inhalt:** Sind alle Punkte aus Abschnitt 2 in deiner Geschichte enthalten?

b) **Sprache**: Enthält deine Story z.B. passende Konnektoren? Ist die Rechtschreibung auch in Ordnung?

5 Jetzt bist du Prüferin oder Prüfer ☺!

Für diese Aufgabe kannst du 15 Punkte bekommen: 7,5 Punkte für den Inhalt und 7,5 Punkte für die Sprache. Dein Text bekommt viele Punkte, wenn du inhaltlich
- die Aufgabe vollständig gelöst hast,
- alle Aspekte eindeutig und zutreffend eingearbeitet hast,
- originelle und ansprechende Ideen verwendet hast,
- den Handlungsverlauf schlüssig und klar dargestellt hast.

Sprachlich hast du geachtet auf
- einen logischen Textaufbau, sodass das Lesen keine Mühe bereitet,
- einen breiten Wortschatz und eine gute Verwendung von Konnektoren,
- eine sichere Verwendung von grammatischer Strukturen,
- die Vermeidung von Fehlern.

Entscheide, wie viele Punkte dein Text verdient und warum.

Punkte: _____

Begründung: _____

Englisch

Abschluss-prüfungs-trainer

Niedersachsen

Lösungen

LÖSUNGEN

TRAINING SECTION: Listening ▶ S. 14–19

Part 1 – Auswahlaufgaben (Multiple choice) mit Bildern
Olivia and Dad
Tipp: **B** *museum, exhibition* **C** *shops, shopping*
Picture C

Part 2 – Auswahlaufgaben (Multiple choice) mit Sätzen
Tim's visit to Krakow
1b) Tipp: *fly, flight, airport, …*
2c) Tipp: *a + b*
3a) Tipp: *verneinte Aussage – NOT the main tourist sites*
4b) Tipp: *Synonym zu making signs = use hands; Antonym zu learnt at school = taught myself*

Part 3 – Notizen anfertigen (Note-taking)
Calgary's skyways (Part 1)
1 *18 kilometres*
2 *4.5 metres*
3 *15 feet above the ground / up in the air*
4a) *less rain and cold*
4b) *safer*
5 *less life at road level / in the streets*

Part 4 – Richtig/Falsch-Aufgaben (True/False)
Calgary's skyways (Part 2)
1 *false* · 2 *true* · 3 *true*

The Tour de Yorkshire
1c) · 2c) · 3b) · 4b) · 5a)

Bob Marley
1 *true* · 2 *true* · 3 *false* 4 *false* · 5 *true* · 6 *true* · 7 *false* · 8 *false*

Top of the Rock
1 *Central Park*
2 *8 am*
3 *No waiting time / No queue*
4 *34 dollars*
5 *can visit twice in one day / on the same day*
6 *wear warm clothes*

TRAINING SECTION: Reading ▶ S. 20–28

Auswahlaufgaben (Multiple choice)
Australia's Stolen Generations
1b) · 2a)
Tipp: Das Antonym im Text zu *forced to stay* in 1c) ist *had to leave*.
Tipp: *… began to take children away / … they were given foods …*
Tipp: 2c) ist nicht die richtige Lösung, weil es keine verneinte Aussage ist: *They were not allowed to speak their own language* ist das Gegenteil von *They had to speak their own language*.

Richtig/Falsch-Aufgaben (True/False)
Tipp: Sammelbegriff: *culture*
Lösung: *true*

Zuordnungsaufgaben (Matching)
Activities for Karen, Jack and Olivia
1 E · 2 D · 3 C
Tipp zu A: *Jack möchte mit Kindern arbeiten.*
Tipp zu B: *Olivia sucht ein neues Betätigungsfeld.*

Richtig/Falsch-Aufgaben mit Zeilenangaben (True/False with line reference)
Kasun
Tipp zu Satz 2: *Kasun hat Angst, geschlagen zu werden.*
Tipp zu Satz 3: *Kasun stottert und redet zu schnell.*
1 *false: lines 2–3* 2 *true: lines 6–7* 3 *true: lines 10–12*

Part 1 – Richtig/Falsch-Aufgaben (True/False)
What's on?
1 *false* · 2 *true* · 3 *false* · 4 *true* · 5 *true*

Part 2 – Richtig/Falsch-Aufgaben (True/False)
Work practice assignments
1 C · 2 G · 3 B · 4 H · 5 E

Part 3 – Auswahlaufgaben (Multiple choice)
Filming in New Zealand
1 a) · 2 b) · 3 a) · 4 d)

Part 4 – Richtig/Falsch-Aufgaben mit Zeilenangaben (True/False with line reference)
The Isle of Man TT race
1 *false: lines 8–9* · 2 *true: lines 10–12* · 3 *true: lines 18–19* · 4 *false: lines 27–29* · 5 *false: lines 33–38*

TRAINING SECTION: Mediating ▶ S. 29–33

Tipp zu **1 Die Ausgangssituation:**
Das nigerianische Mädchen Adelola spricht Englisch und der Fußballtrainer spricht Deutsch.

Tipps zu **2 Mediating von gesprochenen Sätzen:**
c) eine Frage
Wir hatten bisher immer getrennte Mannschaften für Jungen und andere für Mädchen.
Wir haben aber Pläne für gemischte Mannschaften. Wir denken da an ein neues Turnier mit gemischten Mannschaften nächstes Jahr. Ich hole mal eine Broschüre dazu.

Lösungsbeispiel:
You (1) Spielen im Verein Mädchen und Jungen zusammen?
You (2) *They have different teams for boys and girls – but they'll have mixed teams soon.*
You (3) *A new competition for mixed teams is planned for next year. The trainer is getting a brochure about it.*

Tipps zu **3 Mediating von einem Text:**
1 drei Fragen
2 She would like to know when the first mixed teams will play, whether she is old enough to play (she is 16 now), and how teams qualify as mixed teams.
3 Ja, du sollst zwei Infos aussuchen, die Adelola interessieren könnten.

Lösungsbeispiel:
You (4) *September next year*
You (5) *she will be too old (17 next year)*

You (6) *at least four boys and four girls in a team*

Für **(7)** und **(8)** kannst du zwei von diesen drei Antwortmöglichkeiten verwenden:
- *young people of Adelola's age will be able to play in future,*
- *young people of Adelola's age can help train the younger players,*
- *young people of Adelola's age can help with organisation of the competition.*

Tipp zur Broschüre: *vielleicht in späteren Jahren*

Tipps zu **4 Mediating mit Pronomenwechsel:**
Du sagst: Er/Sumon ist gespannt, ob …
Du sagst: Er/Sumon mag die Wurst.

Lösungsbeispiel:
You (1) Axel wants to buy us a vegetarian Currywurst. He thinks you'll really like the sauce.
You (2) Sumon bedankt sich. Er ist gespannt, ob die Soße so schmeckt wie eine aus Bangladesch.
You (3) Er mag die Wurst, findet die Soße aber ungewohnt.

(4) *19th century / about 100 to 200 years ago*
(5) *made from dried / not fresh herbs/spices/ingredients*
(6) *after World War 2 / soon after 1945*

Für **(7)** und **(8)** kannst du zwei von diesen drei Antwortmöglichkeiten verwenden:
- *most owners of Indian restaurants in GB are in fact Bengladeshi*
- *dried spices used instead of range of fresh spices in Asia*
- *the first Currywurst sauce was a mix of two British (not Asian) sauces*

TRAINING SECTION: Writing ▶ S. 34–40

The 50 word text

1 Die Arbeitsanweisungen
Tipp: Markiere:
- *Give some general information about your town/village.*
- *Say what life is like there for young people.*
- *Say what you like best about your town/village.*

4 Sprache

> Our town **has** some good things and some bad things too. For example, **it has** a really modern sports centre with an amazing **swimming** pool. I swim **there** every week. But on the other hand our town **doesn't** have enough cafes or places **where** young people can meet.

The 80 word text

3 Inhalt und Sprache
Blau markiert sind Stellen, die den Inhalt der Aufgabe erfüllen. Grau markiert sind Nebensätze.

> Last weekend I went with my friend Sam on a camping trip in the mountains. Dave had wanted to come too, but he didn't have time because he had so much homework. We hiked along muddy valleys, we climbed steep hills and in the evening we cooked on an open fire. Although the weather was awful, it was great fun. The wet nights weren't great, but it was a great feeling when I stood on the highest mountain that I had ever climbed!

3d) Wortschatz
- Verben im *simple past*: *went, didn't have, had, hiked, climbed, cooked, was, weren't, stood*
- Adjektive: *muddy, steep, open, awful, great, wet, highest*
- *linking words* (Konnektoren): *but, because, although, when, that*

The 120 word text: Creative writing

3 Sprache
had never wanted: **B** (Vielfalt an grammatischen Strukturen) · *when he got*: **F** (Nebensätze) · *Still*: **C** (unterschiedliche Satzanfänge) · *Would he make some stupid mistakes? Would the other workers be nice to him?*: **E** (Fragesätze) · *suddenly*: **A** (breiter Wortschatz) · *hands and knees*: **A** (breiter Wortschatz) · *when the door opened*: **F** (Nebensätze) · *enormous*: **A** (breiter Wortschatz) · *"Well, good morning. Have you lost something?"*: **D** (in den Text integrierter Dialog)

MUSTERPRÜFUNG 1: Listening ▶ S. 41–44

Part 1 – Questions 1–4
1 A · 2 B · 3 B · 4 A

Part 2 – Questions 5–10
Bo-Kaap – a special district in Cape Town
5 b) · 6 c) · 7 b) · 8 c) · 9 a) · 10 c)

Part 3 – Questions 11–16
A presentation about William Shakespeare
11 poems and *(38) plays*
12 *April 1564*
13 *1606*
14 *born*
15 *student*
16 *1997*

Part 4 – Questions 17–23
A great language experience
17 *false* · 18 *false* · 19 *true* · 20 *true* · 21 *false* · 22 *true* · 23 *false*

LÖSUNGEN

MUSTERPRÜFUNG 1: Reading ▶ S. 45–50

Part 1 – Questions 1–5
1 *true* · 2 *false* · 3 *false* · 4 *true* · 5 *true*

Part 2 – Questions 6–11
6 E · 7 G · 8 C · 9 B · 10 H · 11 A

Part 3 – Questions 12–18
High-rise living in Britain
12 c) · 13 b) · 14 c) · 15 b) · 16 a) · 17 b) · 18 d)

Part 4 – Questions 19–23
The Everglades
19 *false: lines 3–5* · 20 *true: lines 10–13* · 21 *true: lines 15–16* · 22 *false: lines 20–22* · 23 *false: lines 27–29*

MUSTERPRÜFUNG 1: Mediating ▶ S. 51–52

Lösungsbeispiel:
- **You (1)** *Sie möchte zum Rathaus. Was kostet das?*
- **You (2)** *2.80 euros – but it's cheaper if you buy a ticket from a machine next time.*
- **You (3)** *Entschuldigen Sie, kennen Sie zufällig das Jugendzentrum Hegeda?*
- **You (4)** *Go round the corner, and it's opposite / on the far side of the road.*
- **You (5)** *help write a CV and help look for a job*
- **You (6/7)** *help in cafe for younger children / help repair bicycles*
- **You (8/9)** *games like table tennis, billiard and table football / German as a foreign language / cafe on Wednesday 4–6 pm*

MUSTERPRÜFUNG 1: Writing ▶ S. 52–53

> **Hinweis zu den Lösungsvorschlägen beim Schreiben:**
> Für kürzere und mittlere Schreibaufgaben (Texte von 50 oder 80 Wörtern Länge) werden englischsprachige Lösungsbeispiele angeboten, die als Orientierungshilfe dienen. Es sind aber natürlich auch inhaltlich andere Lösungen denkbar. Wegen der möglichen Bandbreite an unterschiedlichen Lösungen bei den längeren Schreibaufgaben (120 Wörter) werden für diese Teilaufgaben nur die inhaltlichen Aspekte knapp auf Deutsch skizziert. Siehe ausführlich dazu auch die Hinweise zur Bewertung von Inhalt und Sprache auf S. 34. Generell gilt, dass die folgenden Aspekte in deinem Text berücksichtigt sein sollten, um die volle Punktzahl zu bekommen:
> - Du machst wenige Wiederholungen und schweifst nicht vom Thema ab.
> - Dein Text lässt sich leicht lesen.
> - Dein Text ist klar formuliert und logisch aufgebaut. Du verwendest Bindewörter (Konnektoren) wie *because, but, so* etc.
> - Du verwendest einen vielseitigen Wortschatz und idiomatische Wendungen, z.B. *make a difference*.
> - Du bist sicher in der Verwendung verschiedener grammatischer Strukturen.
> - Auch wenn bei komplizierten Sätzen vereinzelte Wortschatz- oder Grammatikfehler vorkommen, versteht man, was du sagen willst.
>
> **Tipp:** Zeig deinen Text doch einem Mitschüler oder einer Mitschülerin und lasse ihn oder sie beurteilen, ob du diese Aspekte berücksichtigt hast. Oder sprich deinen Lehrer oder deine Lehrerin an – die können es am allerbesten beurteilen.

Writing – Set 1
Part 1 – Asking for information
Lösungsbeispiel:

Hi,
We are four people, and we'd like to stay in your youth hostel for three nights from Friday 22nd July.
Can we buy vegetarian food at the hostel?
We like rock-climbing and pony trekking. Can you please send me information about these sports in or near Whitby?
Many thanks.
(name)

Part 2 – Writing about a journey
Lösungsbeispiel:

Hi James,
I'm in New York! The journey was a nightmare. First I overslept and nearly missed my train. Then the flight was delayed, and in New York there was a strike, so I couldn't get to my hotel by subway – I had to take a taxi.
But everything is OK now.
Best wishes,
(name)

Part 3 – An online discussion
Die Aufgabe ist vollständig gelöst, indem du deine Meinung zu den Vor- und Nachteilen des Reisens gegenüber Fernsehen und Internet begründet darstellst.

Writing – Set 2
Part 1 – A letter of complaint
Deine Reklamationsmail beinhaltet:
- Angaben zum gekauften Gegenstand (Gegenstand/Datum des Kaufs/Preis),
- eine kurze Beschreibung des Defekts,
- eine Bitte, was jetzt passieren soll.

Lösungsbeispiel:

Hi,
I bought a fitness band from you on 15th December and paid £24.99 by credit card. You sent it on 16th December.
When I first put the fitness band on, it worked fine. But when I tried to recharge the battery, I have found that the battery wouldn't charge.
May I therefore ask you to please send me a replacement battery or charger? I can send you the old battery or charger if you wish.
Best wishes and thank you,
(name)

Part 2 – A blog entry
The best day in my life
Dein Blogeintrag beinhaltet:
- die Beschreibung eines besonderen Tages,
- die Beschreibung deiner Gefühle,
- eine Begründung, warum der Tag so besonders war.

MUSTERPRÜFUNG 2: Listening ▶ S. 55–57

Part 1 – Questions 1–4
1 A · 2 A · 3 B · 4 C

Part 2 – Questions 5–10
First job
5 a) · 6 c) · 7 b) · 8 a) · 9 b) · 10 c)

Part 3 – Questions 11–16
Concorde
11 over *twice the speed of sound*
12 *two hours and 53 minutes*
13 *Europe to North America / North America to Europe*
14 *too much fuel*
15 *not enough passengers*
16 *(bad/fatal) accident / crashed*

Part 4 – Questions 17–23
Cricket in India
17 *false* · 18 *true* · 19 *false* · 20 *false* · 21 *true* ·
22 *true* · 23 *false*

MUSTERPRÜFUNG 2: Reading ▶ S. 58–63

Part 1 – Questions 1–5
1 *true* · 2 *false* · 3 *true* · 4 *false* · 5 *true*

Part 2 – Questions 6–11
6 D · 7 H · 8 F · 9 B · 10 G · 11 E

Part 3 – Questions 12–18
Life in South Africa today
12 c) · 13 d) · 14 a) · 15 b) · 16 b) · 17 a) · 18 c)

Part 4 – Questions 19–24
My three favourite tourist attractions in Brighton
19 *false: lines 11–13* · 20 *true: lines 20–21* · 21 *false: lines 31–33* · 22 *false: lines 65–66* · 23 *true: lines 71–72*

MUSTERPRÜFUNG 2: Mediating ▶ S. 64–65

You (1) Er möchte wissen, ob es hier Deutschkurse für Ausländer gibt?
You (2) *No, there aren't any courses here, but there are German courses in Hannover.*
You (3) Wissen Sie, wo man in Hannover Auskunft über Deutschkurse für Ausländer bekommt?
You (4) *You could maybe get information at the town hall.*
You (5) *She has a brochure with a place that could be useful. You can take the brochure with you.*
You (6/7) *It's open Monday to Friday and it has information/ advice for people from abroad. / You can have lunch: easy way of meeting people. / They can speak Arabic. / If you can't go there, they will come to your house.*

MUSTERPRÜFUNG 2: Writing ▶ S. 65–66

Writing – Set 1
Part 1 – Giving information
Lösungsbeispiel:
*Hi,
My school is a big building in the middle of Wolfsburg. We have classrooms, three science laboratories and lots of long corridors. We don't have any playing fields.
On some days lessons end at 1 pm, but on other days we have lessons in the afternoon. That's why we have a school canteen.
(name)*

Part 2 – Writing about a problem
Lösungsbeispiel:
*Hi James,
It snowed yesterday and I couldn't go to school using the cycle lane. So I tried to go with mum by car, but the car wouldn't move! In the end I went by bus. I got to school one hour late because of the traffic. Well, I wasn't sorry!
(name)*

Part 3 – An online discussion
Dein Diskussionsbeitrag beinhaltet:
• eine Erläuterung, warum Sport wichtig ist,
• deine eigenen Sporterfahrungen,
• deine Meinung zu der Frage, warum die Menschen zu wenig Sport treiben.

Writing – Set 2
Part 1 – A letter to a town council
Dein Brief beinhaltet:
• eine Schilderung dessen, was das Radfahren in der englischen Stadt gefährlich gemacht hat,
• einen Vergleich mit der Situation für Radfahrer an deinem Heimatort,
• einen Vorschlag, wie die Stadtverwaltung die Situation für Radfahrer verbessern könnte.
Lösungsbeispiel:
*Dear Sir/Madam,
I found cycling here very dangerous. Bikes have to use the roads. There isn't enough room for the bikes on the road and it's dangerous when cars turn.
In Germany we have separate cycle lanes. That's much safer. And cars have to stop for cyclists when they turn.
I think you should provide cycle lanes and also covered cycle stands so that bikes don't get wet when it rains. Then more people would cycle. That would help.
Yours sincerely,
(name)*

Part 2 – A competition
My favourite of all places
Dein Wettbewerbsbeitrag beinhaltet:
• die Nennung und Beschreibung deines Lieblingsortes,
• die Schilderung, wie du von diesem Platz erfahren hast bzw. was du dort schon erlebt oder gemacht hast,
• die Erklärung, warum dir dieser Ort so viel bedeutet.

MUSTERPRÜFUNG 3: Listening ▶ S. 68–70

Part 1 – Questions 1–4
1 B · 2 C · 3 B · 4 A

Part 2 – Questions 5–10
A presentation about Wales
5 b) · 6 c) · 7 c) · 8 a) · 9 b) · 10 c)

LÖSUNGEN

Part 3 – Questions 11–17
St Kilda
11 *caught / ate birds*
12 *farmed land*
13 *(currents in) the sea*
14 *young people left*
15 *men died in the war*
16 the people of St Kilda *left the island.*
17 can stay in *a campsite.*

Part 4 – Questions 18–25
The D of E *expedition*
18 *true* · 19 *true* · 20 *false* · 21 *false* · 22 *true* · 23 *false* · 24 *false* · 25 *true*

MUSTERPRÜFUNG 3: Reading ▶ S. 71–76

Part 1 – Questions 1–5
1 *true* · 2 *false* · 3 *false* · 4 *false* · 5 *true*

Part 2 – Questions 6–11
6 A · 7 E · 8 G · 9 H · 10 D · 11 F

Part 3 – Questions 12–16
Good health in Australia?
12 d) · 13 b) · 14 b) · 15 c) · 16 d)

Part 4 – Questions 17–21
The Mousetrap
17 *true: lines 2–6* · 18 *false: lines 14–16* · 19 *false: lines 21–22* · 20 *false: lines 30–32* · 21 *true: lines 42–44*

MUSTERPRÜFUNG 3: Mediating ▶ S. 77–78

You (1) Spieler mit jeder Erfahrung können sich melden.
You (2) Am Samstagvormittag und an drei Tagen in den Oster-, Sommer- und Weihnachtsferien.
You (3) 50 Pfund pro Tag, oder 45 Pfund, wenn man sich früh anmeldet.
You (4) Man kann sich für Ermäßigungen bewerben.
You (5) *How old must/may/can the players be?*
You (6) *Can my friend borrow a trumpet to practise?*
You (7) *Are the orchestras preparing for a concert?*
You (8) *Is it OK if my friend doesn't speak English so well?*

MUSTERPRÜFUNG 3: Writing ▶ S. 78–79

Writing – Set 1
Part 1 – Answering a letter
Lösungsbeispiel:
Dear George,
Thank you for your card and for the money. It was very kind of you!
Last week my phone stopped working. I took it to a shop, but it can't be repaired. But with your money, together with money from Mum, I can buy a new one. Thank you!
(name)

Part 2 – A review for a hotel
Lösungsbeispiel:
The Hotel Adria is terrible! When we arrived, we had to wait for two hours because our room wasn't ready. And when we tried to have a shower we found that the shower didn't work. The food is OK, but the drinks are very expensive. And the receptionists aren't very helpful.
(name)

Part 3 – A blog
Social media and the generations
Dein Blogeintrag beinhaltet:
- deine persönlichen Erfahrungen mit den sozialen Medien,
- deine Erfahrungen, wie und ob ältere Leute die sozialen Medien nutzen,
- deine Meinung zu der Frage, ob durch die sozialen Medien Probleme zwischen den Generationen entstehen.

Writing – Set 2
Part 1 – An application to take part in an event
Deine E-Mail beinhaltet:
- den Grund, warum du mitlaufen möchtest,
- deine Lauferfahrung,
- wie du von dem Lauf erfahren hast,
- wie du zum Start kommst,
- eine Frage zum Lauf.

Lösungsbeispiel:
Running is my favourite. I run for fun and also in a club in my home town. And last year I took part in a half marathon in Bielefeld and really enjoyed it. I am staying in England for two weeks and would love to have the opportunity to run here!
Do I have to bring my own drinks or are drinks provided during the run? Is there transport back to the start of the race if I don't complete it?

Part 2 – A picture story
Du kannst wählen, ob du die Bildgeschichte in der ersten Person erzählen magst, oder aber auch aus der Sicht einer der abgebildeten Personen. Deine Geschichte beinhaltet die Beschreibung aller Bilder und hat sowohl eine passende Überschrift als auch ein passendes Ende.

Tipps für die Prüfung

Prüfungsvorbereitung

- **Beginne rechtzeitig mit dem Lernen und mache dir einen Lernplan**, bei dem du auch Wiederholungsphasen einplanst. Starte mit Aufgaben, die dir im Unterricht noch schwerfallen. Hake ab, was du bereits erledigt hast.
- **Überlege dir, wo du im Englischen noch grundsätzliche Probleme oder Lücken hast** (z. B. Grammatikprobleme, die immer wieder auftreten). Diese Themen kannst du dann mit den interaktiven Übungen auf www.scook.de gezielt noch einmal wiederholen.
- **Mache dich mit dem Ablauf der Prüfung und mit allen Aufgabenformaten vertraut.** Plane im Vorfeld, wie viel Zeit du für jeden Prüfungsteil und für die Kontrolle zur Verfügung hast.
- **Schreibe dir auf, wann und wo die Prüfung stattfindet**, und plane etwas mehr Zeit für den Weg ein als sonst.
- **Lege alle Materialien am Vorabend der Prüfung bereit** (z. B. funktionstüchtige Stifte, Uhr; Smartphones sind in der Regel nicht erlaubt!).
- **Achte auf ausreichend Schlaf und ein gutes Frühstück.**

Wenn du dich gut vorbereitet hast, kannst du selbstbewusst in die Prüfung gehen!

Während der Prüfung

- **Behalte die Zeit im Blick!** Am besten legst du während der Prüfung eine Uhr auf den Tisch und schaust von Zeit zu Zeit darauf. Wenn du an einer Aufgabe festhängst, gehe lieber erstmal zur nächsten Frage weiter. Nimm dir am Ende einige Minuten Zeit, um deine Antworten noch einmal durchzugehen.
- **Lies die Aufgabenstellung gründlich durch**, bevor du mit der Bearbeitung beginnst. Manchmal enthält eine Aufgabe mehrere Teilaspekte. Markiere sie und übersetze sie dir zur Sicherheit in deine Muttersprache.
- **Nutze deine Chance!** Auch wenn du unsicher bist, ob die Lösung stimmt, so ist es ratsam, die Aufgabe trotzdem zu bearbeiten. So hast du zumindest eine Chance, dass es richtig ist. Kreuzt du keine Lösung an oder lässt die Lücke leer, so bekommst du auf jeden Fall null Punkte.
- **Mache dir bei Schreibaufgaben Notizen, wenn du gut in der Zeit liegst.** Sie können dir helfen, deine Gedanken zu ordnen und deinen Text sinnvoll zu strukturieren. Beachte aber, dass nur dein endgültiger Text in die Bewertung eingeht.
- **Gib deinen Texten eine gute Struktur mit Einleitung, Hauptteil und Schluss.** Beginne jeden neuen Textteil mit einem neuen Absatz.
- **Formuliere klare Sätze.** Vermeide es, komplizierte deutsche Sätze wortwörtlich ins Englische zu übersetzen. Formuliere möglichst mit deinen eigenen Worten, es sei denn, die Aufgabenstellung verlangt ein Zitat aus dem Text (z. B. „Quote from the text.", „Give examples from the text.").
- **Kontrolliere am Ende**, was du geschrieben hast. Achte besonders auf Vollständigkeit, die Rechtschreibung, die Zeitformen deiner Verben und den Satzbau.

Wir wünschen dir viel Erfolg für deine Prüfung!

Mündliche Prüfung

Speaking about yourself

a) Questions + short answers
   Answer these questions about yourself.
   1. Hello. How are you feeling today?
   2. Can you tell me your name, please, and how you spell it?
   3. Do you have brothers and sisters?
   4. What's your favourite subject at school?
   5. How long have you been at this school?
   6. Can you tell me what you usually eat for lunch?

b) Questions + longer answers
   Give longer answers to these questions.
   1. Tell me something about your school. Do you like it here?
   2. What do you usually do in the evenings and at the weekend?
   3. Please tell me something about the region where you live.
   4. What are you going to do when you leave school?

c) Picture prompt

Talk about the picture.
– What can you see?
– Talk about their feelings.

d) Discussion

In this part of the test you are talking to each other.
Imagine that your school is running a project on how to help cut pollution and protect the environment in your town.
Talk to each other about what projects the school should support.
On your cards, there are some ideas, but you can suggest other things too.
Talk about how useful these projects would be for young people in your town and try to agree about the three most useful ones. You have about five minutes. Start when you are ready.

Candidate 1
- More cycling lanes
- Solar panels on school roof
- Less waste in school canteen
- Use school land to grow vegetables
- Recycled paper at school
- Any more ideas?

Candidate 2
- Locally-grown food in school canteen
- Recycling containers in school yard
- Turn down the heating
- No car park for teachers
- More places for bikes at school
- Any more ideas?

Schriftliche Prüfung

Bearbeitungszeit: 120 min

I. Listening

Part 1 – Questions 1–4

You will hear four short conversations.
For each question there are three pictures and a short recording.
Choose the correct picture and put a tick in the box below it.

1 Where did Sabrina go last weekend?

2 What activity will Noah and his friends probably do at the school fair?

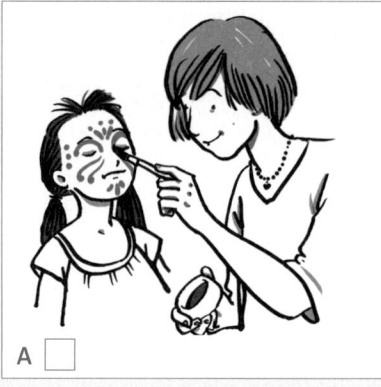  

3 When should Mrs Taylor be at the dentist?

4 Where's the post office?

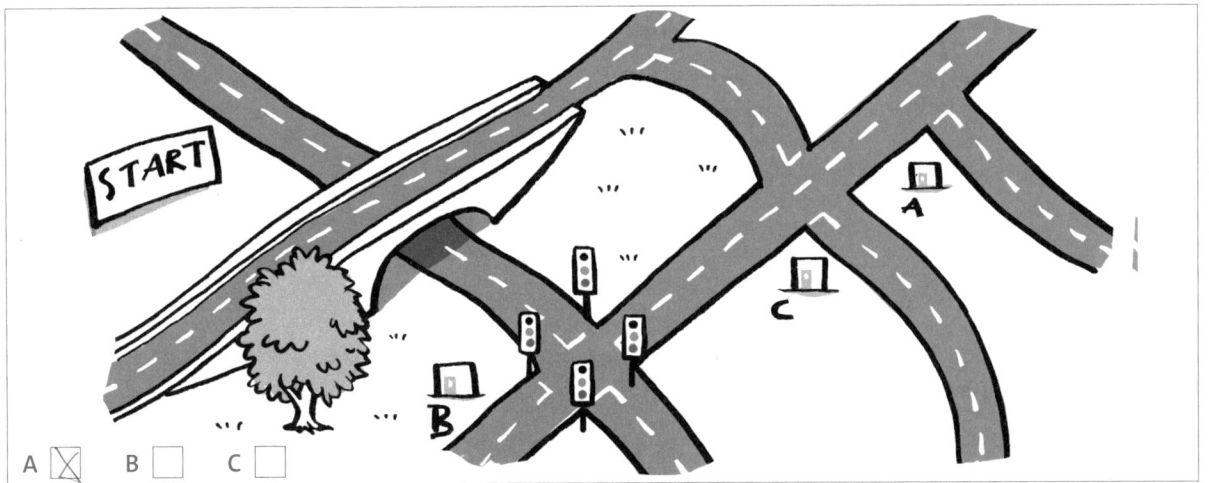

A ☒ B ☐ C ☐

Part 2 – Questions 5–10

Bo-Kaap – a special district in Cape Town

Listen to the tourist guide giving a tour of the Bo-Kaap district in Cape Town, South Africa. For questions 5–10 tick the correct box a), b) or c).

5 The Bo-Kaap mosque was built ...
   a) ☐ a hundred years ago.
   b) ☒ at the end of the 18th century.
   c) ☐ in 1974.

6 The people who ruled Cape Town back then ...
   a) ☐ were Asian.
   b) ☐ built the Bo-Kaap mosque.
   c) ☒ were Europeans.

A street in Bo-Kaap

7 Over one million people in South Africa ...
   a) ☐ are Muslim.
   b) ☒ are Asian.
   c) ☐ are from Bo-Kaap.

8 The Bo-Kaap Museum ...
   a) ☐ was built in 1964.
   b) ☐ has exhibitions, but no furniture.
   c) ☒ gives information about the Asian population of Cape Town.

9 What is so special in this part of Wale Street is that ...
   a) ☒ the houses are brightly painted.
   b) ☐ the people speak so many different languages.
   c) ☐ there are so many different shops.

10 The people who live in Wale Street today ...
    a) ☐ are a more unified community than ever before.
    b) ☐ are even less ethnically mixed than they were before.
    c) ☒ don't know their neighbours as well as people used to before.

Part 3 – Questions 11–16

A presentation about William Shakespeare

During a visit to a school in England, you listen to a presentation about William Shakespeare by two English students.
Listen to the students.
Complete the notes by filling the gaps 11–16.

William Shakespeare is famous because he wrote	11	poems and plays 38
He was born in	12	April 1564
He died in Stratford-upon-Avon in	13	1606
In Stratford-upon-Avon you can visit the building where Shakespeare was	14	born
And you can visit the building where Shakespeare sat as a	15	student
The Globe Theatre in London opened in	16	1997

Part 4 – Questions 17–23

A great language experience

Look at the seven sentences for this part.
You will hear a radio interview in a series about great language experiences.
The interview is with Paul, an English teenager, who travelled to France with his friend Phil.
For questions 17–23 decide whether each sentence is true or false.
Put a tick in the correct box 'true' or 'false'.

		true	false
17	Paul has always been interested in speaking and learning languages.		✗
18	At first Paul didn't really want to go on a cycling holiday in France with Phil because he didn't really like Phil very much.		✗
19	When Phil asked the way in Calais, it was a positive experience.	✗	
20	In Calais Paul looked forward to sharing a dormitory with two guys from Serbia.	✗	
21	Paul did not understand Filip, the Serb boy, so he used a dictionary.		✗
22	Filip never stopped trying to communicate till Paul understood the whole sentence.	✗	
23	The experience made Paul realize that you have to be able to speak a foreign language perfectly if you want to communicate.		✗

II. Reading

Part 1 – Questions 1–5

Read the texts below. Then read the statements (1–5).
Decide whether the statements are true or false.
Then tick (✓) the correct box.

Monica House Nursery is here to help all mothers with their newborn babies.

We have only been in the childcare business for two years, but already we have an enviable reputation for providing a warm and friendly atmosphere in which your child can learn through play.

Open Monday to Friday 7.30 am to 6.30 pm (term-time only).

Please do not hesitate to contact us.
Phone: 01394 269021
Email: enquiries@monicahouse.co.uk

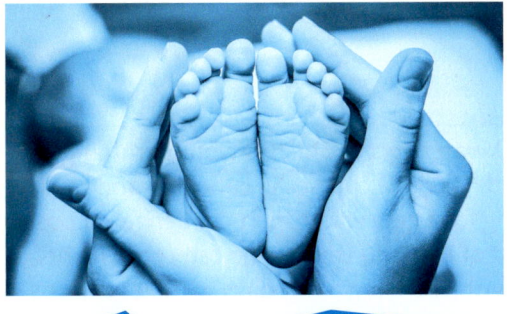

GP Intensive Crash Driving Courses

Getting your driving licence by taking weekly lessons can last about a year or so – but take one of our crash driving courses and you could have your driving licence at the end of the week!

With our *Pass in a Week* course, you'll be driving six hours a day and you'll take your test on the sixth day. And if you fail your first test, we'll pay for your second one!

Note: The normal waiting time for a driving test is 6–8 weeks if you book it yourself – but we guarantee you a test within six days of starting your course.

For more information, please phone 05923 672 071 and ask for Gary.

KCS – Kevin's Cleaning Services

I will happily do your cleaning for you, from the daily washing up, hoovering and tidying to thorough cleaning of your kitchen (including all appliances), toilets and bathroom.
And to give you peace of mind, the first clean will be completely free if you book a weekly service.
I really enjoy my work and have a reputation among friends, family and long-standing customers for my excellent work.
I charge £9 per hour.

Puppy King Supreme

... are proud to offer your pet a premium service at a competitive price.

Bring your pet to us for professional puppy grooming, nail clipping and hygiene clips. All grooming includes a wash, blow dry and tidy up.

All our staff are fully qualified and insured. Prices available on our website. Please visit Puppykingsupreme.com

		true	false
1	Kevin will not only clean the kitchen, but also the oven, fridge, microwave, etc.	☐	☐
2	The nursery can look after a two-week-old child in the last week of July and last week of December.	☐	☐
3	Learning to drive with a GP Crash Course can take about a year.	☐	☐
4	If you learn to drive with a GP Crash Course, you don't have to wait so long as usual to get a date for the driving test.	☐	☐
5	You have to search online to find how much it costs to have a pet washed at *Puppy King Supreme*.	☐	☐

Part 2 – Questions 6–11

Decide which of the holiday activities described in the texts (A–H) is the most suitable for the teenagers below (6–11).

6	Harry's favourite possession is his 24-gear, front and rear suspension mountain bike, and he's out on it most weekends. He loves the challenge of cycling along rough mountain trails – the rougher and steeper, the better. And he doesn't mind carrying his bike over the rougher bits if necessary.
7	Rosanna loves all water sports. She has won swimming competitions, and has done courses in canoeing and kayaking. Now she is looking for a new water sport challenge – if possible in the south-west of England so that she can combine her activity holiday with spending a few days with her cousins in Plymouth.
8	Hassan has been a water rat since he was small. Back stroke, breast stroke, crawl – he is a master of them all. And still he wants to improve his swimming skills, for example by improving his butterfly style. If he can progress enough – who knows – maybe one day he'll become a swimming coach, or even compete in Team GB?
9	Yvonne was 12 when she first learned to ride a bike – but she has never looked back. She loves the wind in her hair, and loves seeing the countryside while pedalling hard through it. She'll happily carry a tent and other heavy equipment in her panniers, so she prefers to avoid steep climbs.

10		Steve's favourite hobby is cycling, and his lightweight drop-handlebar racing bike is his pride and joy. He is a member of a cycling team and has done well in cycle races in a number of local competitions. His ambition is to take part in an international competition such as the *Tour de Yorkshire*, and he is willing to put in the necessary hours of training.
11		Maria's favourite holidays are at the seaside, although she also loves climbing mountains. She has no fear of heights, and loves canyoning – a sport in which you make your way down a narrow rocky gorge, sometimes jumping from rock to rock, sometimes wading through the water or even swimming in it.

A   Coasteering is the new fun sport that combines the best of the sea with the best of the mountains. Wearing wetsuits to keep warm and helmets to keep safe, we use rocky Pembrokeshire coast as our playground. We scramble over rocks, walk through water, and do cliff jumps into the sea – jumps of 10 metres or more! It's so much fun that sometimes, if we're lucky, even the seals come and join us!

B   Do you like your cycling a little smoother? Then join us for long-distance cycling trips on the Tran-spennine Trail, the Tissington Trail and other routes that make use of old railway lines. These trails use the old railway bridges and tunnels, so there is less pedalling up steep hills. We do both day and weekend trips.

C   *Swim UK* organizes courses at all levels. We help complete beginners to overcome their fears and help experienced swimmers to develop and maximise their skills. And we also offer specialist courses for divers, life savers and those wishing to become swimming teachers. We run courses at pools up and down the country – there's probably one near you!

D   Come sea kayaking in the beautiful south-west of England! Based near Plymouth, we were founded over 15 years ago. We know every inch of the area, which is probably one of the best in the UK for sea kayaking. We offer day expeditions, 3-day expeditions and 10-day expeditions for every ability, and provide quality equipment including lightweight paddles, dry bags for personal belongings and either one-piece paddle suits or cags and trousers, as you prefer. Alternatively, you are welcome to use your own equipment.

E   If you're into all-terrain off-roading, we have just the right circuits for you – from gentle slopes to strenuous climbs and dizzying descents, from purpose-made off-road cycling tracks to circuits that take you over rocks, through rivers and swamps. Bring your own bike or hire one from us – just as you like.

F   Enjoy riding a bike? Then upgrade to motorcycling and you'll enjoy those steep climbs. We can train you to ride any size bike or scooter. We offer training courses at all levels, beginning with the Compulsory Basic Training (CBT) test which, by law, you must complete before biking on your own. Don't think of it as a driving test – the CBT can be good fun, and you may even make a friend or two!

G   Whether you are experienced or completely new to surfing, a course at our Surf School at Polzeath in Cornwall will allow you to make maximum progress in the time that you have available. We'll teach you all the basic surfing techniques, water safety and other surfing knowledge you need to enjoy your surfing safely. Three and five day courses available.

H The 6000-seat velodrome where British cyclists won gold at the London 2012 Olympic Games is the fastest track in the world – and it's open for you! Everyone can cycle here, and you don't even need a bike – you can hire everything you need. We can teach you the art of speed cycling, or if you're more ambitious, why not register for our four-day professional cyclist course?

Part 3 – Questions 12–18

Read the text and then tick (✓) the correct statement.
There is only one correct solution per statement.

High-rise living in Britain

The following text is from the lifestyle section of a British newspaper.

Tower block in London

High-rise apartment blocks have long had a bad press in Britain. People think of the 1960s tower blocks that were usually built for people in lower-paid jobs. The flats were small and the entrances were dark and dirty, full of litter and graffiti. The lifts kept breaking down. That was no joke if you lived on the 10th floor and arrived home with your week's shopping or a child in a wheelchair. The general view was that people only lived in such buildings if they had no alternative. In several cities, councils destroyed some of their high-rise apartment blocks.

Of course, the tower blocks have always had their fans, above all because of the amazing views that residents often have from their flats. In addition, people in tower blocks often say that they feel safer than in a house. That's because nobody can climb through the window of a flat on the 16th floor: in fact, nobody can even look in, so you don't have to draw your curtains at night. And the flats are largely free from mice, ants and spiders. These voices, however, were long in the minority. Not any more.

Look at the skyline of most British cities today and you'll see that apartment blocks are going up all around you. Why this sudden popularity of flats? One reason is that with land becoming more and more expensive, houses are simply costing too much for many people. Building taller, it seems, is the only way of building cheaper homes. And the new trend for flats also reflects a change in lifestyle. In the past, a house and garden was seen as an ideal, but these days many people get home late from work – so they have no time for garden work. Instead, they prefer to have a few plants on an easily-managed balcony.

What's more, the apartments that have been built in the last few years attract people on good incomes. They are large and airy. CCTV cameras keep the entrances safe, and companies are employed to clean the corridors and maintain the lifts. Some of these modern flats are built as 'pods' – that is to say, each flat is built as a self-contained unit, with bathrooms and kitchen equipped to a high standard, and the pods are then simply placed one on top of the other. This is often less costly than traditional building techniques, and customers can make their choice of equipment as they would do if they were buying a car.

It is true that families with children still usually prefer to live in a house with a front door, a back door and a garden. Parents can keep an eye on their children, and it's often easier to get to know your neighbours by chatting over the garden fence than by sharing the lift up the

8th floor. But a recent report has challenged the widely-held view that high-rise blocks offer a less healthy environment.

Experts from the University of Bern in Switzerland found that people who live on the 8th floor or above are likely to live longer than those who live on the lower floors. Those living higher up, they claim, are 40 % less likely to die of lung disease, and 35 % less likely to die from heart disease – partly because walking up more stairs keeps people fitter. There is also less air pollution on the higher floors and people are also less affected by traffic noise.

The British population is expected to grow from about 65 million in 2016 to 75 million by 2040, so millions of new homes will have to be built. If we want to protect our countryside, we will have to build them in our cities, and as the price of land in cities goes up, it is clear that more people will have to live in flats. The apartment blocks being built today are here to stay.

12 The flats in the 1960s tower blocks …

a) ☐ were not always clean, but at least had good lifts instead of stairs.

b) ☐ were ideal for families with disabled children.

c) ☐ were often not in good condition.

d) ☐ have a good reputation today.

13 Some people felt that flats were …

a) ☐ full of insects.

b) ☐ safer because burglars could not break in so easily.

c) ☐ dangerous because you could fall out of the windows.

d) ☐ too dark when the curtains were closed at night.

14 Flats are becoming more popular again because …

a) ☐ people have more money, so they can pay the higher rents.

b) ☐ people want to live higher off the ground floor.

c) ☐ they can be maintained more easily.

d) ☐ they sometimes have a nice garden.

15 The flats now under construction …

a) ☐ have CCTV cameras inside them to keep people safe.

b) ☐ are often better quality than those built in the 1960s.

c) ☐ tend to be small in size.

d) ☐ are for people who do not earn much money.

16 The flats that are built as pods …

a) ☐ are often cheaper than other flats.

b) ☐ have poor quality kitchens and bathrooms.

c) ☐ can only be used at ground floor level.

d) ☐ means that people can't choose what they want to have in their flats.

17 Living on higher floors in apartment blocks …

a) ☐ is louder.

b) ☐ helps against heart disease.

c) ☐ is dangerous because the air is dirtier.

d) ☐ is bad for you because you have to climb so many stairs.

18 The writer says that more British people will have to live in flats in the future because …

a) ☐ the population is rising.

b) ☐ so many homes need to be built.

c) ☐ fewer people want to live in the countryside.

d) ☐ land is becoming more expensive.

Part 4 – Questions 19 – 23

Read the text and then tick (✓) the correct statement.
There is only one correct solution per statement.

The Everglades

The wetlands of the Everglades in the south of the state of Florida are famous for their alligators, snakes, turtles and other wildlife, which tourists can sometimes catch sight of from airboats or from specially-provided hiking trails. Visitor centres show alligators feeding and inform tourists about how the alligators' environment is endangered.

In fact, the Everglades are facing huge environmental issues. Its lakes and rivers are polluted by dirty waste water from the city of Miami. And pets released into the Everglades by inhabitants of the city have become a danger to the original wildlife.

But the biggest headache of all is that the wetlands are drying out. This is partly because, in the 1960ies, the slow-flowing Kissimmee River was replaced by a dead straight canal that takes the water away too quickly. And what

makes it worse is that the U.S. Highway 41, which was completed in 1928, cuts through 275 miles of the Everglades from east to west on a wall of earth. This prevents water from flowing into the southern part of the Everglades.

It has now been decided that parts of the canal will be filled in to allow the water to flow in the slower river. And a mile-long stretch of Highway 41 will be made into a bridge to allow water to pass under it.

		true	false	line(s)
19	Tourists can catch alligators and snakes in the Everglades.	☐	☐	_____
20	The population of Miami is a threat to the Everglades.	☐	☐	_____
21	There is not enough water in the Everglades.	☐	☐	_____
22	Too much water passes from the north to the south of the Everglades as a result of the route of Highway 41.	☐	☐	_____
23	A new bridge over Highway 41 is the solution to the water problem.	☐	☐	_____

III. Mediating

Du bist in der Stadt Lüneburg zu Besuch und fährst mit dem Bus in die Stadt. Ein Mädchen steigt an einer Bushaltestelle ein und versucht mit dem Busfahrer zu reden. Sie spricht aber kein Deutsch und der Busfahrer kein Englisch.
Du bietest an, zu vermitteln.

Mädchen I'm going to a youth centre somewhere near the Town Hall. I don't know what the bus fare is.

You (1) _____

Busfahrer 2,80 Euro. Aber sag ihr bitte, dass sie sich Geld spart, wenn sie sich nächstes Mal den Fahrschein aus dem Automaten an der Haltestelle besorgt.

You (2) _____

Das Mädchen löst eine Fahrkarte und setzt sich neben dich. Sie heißt Grace und kommt aus Malta. Ihr steigt an der Haltestelle beim Rathaus beide aus.

Grace I don't know where the youth centre it. Would you mind asking somebody the way for me? That would be really kind of you. Look at this brochure. It's called the *Jugendzentrum Hegeda*.

You (3) _____

Fußgänger Ja. Sie müssen dort um die Ecke, und dann ist es gleich gegenüber.

You (4) _____

Grace People told me they could help me find a job here. Can you please look at this brochure and tell me what they can do for me?

Du schaust dir die Broschüre (S. 52) an. Gib Grace die relevanten Informationen.

You (5) _____

Grace I like helping out with things. Is there I anything I can do to help here?

You (6/7) *Mache zwei Vorschläge:*

_____

_____

Grace Could this also be a place for my brother and sister? They're 13 and 14.

You (8/9) *Mache zwei passende Verschläge:*

_____

_____

Jugendzentrum Hegeda

Im Jugendzentrum Hegeda können sich Jugendliche von 12 bis 18 Jahren treffen.
Wollt Ihr einfach nur eure Freunde sehen, spielen, klönen oder einfach mal entspannen, könnt Ihr das bei uns tun.

Euch stehen vielfältige Freizeitangebote wie zum Beispiel Tischtennis, Billard oder Tischfußball zur Verfügung sowie Kurse in Deutsch für Ausländer. Mittwochs ist von 16 Uhr bis 18 Uhr Kindercafe.

Älteren Jugendlichen bieten wir Unterstützung bei der Berufsfindung, d.h. beim Bewerbungsschreiben oder bei der Lehrstellensuche.
Wenn ihr Stress, Kummer oder Ärger mit euren Eltern, Geschwistern oder Freunden habt, sind wir für euch da.

Ihr könnt unter Anleitung Fahrräder reparieren, die Küche nutzen und euch am Kindercafe als Organisatoren beteiligen.

Alle Jugendliche von 12 bis 18 werden auch zu unseren *Abenden der internationalen Küche* herzlich eingeladen, an denen junge Menschen aus aller Welt die Küche ihres Landes vorstellen (3,50 Euro Kostenbeitrag). Diese Abende finden ungefähr alle zwei Wochen statt

IV. Writing – Set 1

Part 1 – Asking for information

You are planning a trip to the seaside in Yorkshire, England, with three friends from school. Write a short email to the youth hostel in Whitby.
- Ask to book at the youth hostel, saying when you'll arrive and how long you'll stay.
- Ask if they serve vegetarian food.
- Ask about two outdoor activities that you are interested in.

Write about 50 words.

Whitby

Part 2 – Writing about a journey

Last Tuesday you travelled with a school group to New York and something went wrong.
Write a short email to an English friend. Tell him or her about your journey.
Write about 50 words.
The pictures are only examples of things that went wrong.

Part 3 – An online discussion

You have found an online discussion on the following topic:
You don't have to travel: you can meet the world on TV or on the internet.
Write an entry on this discussion giving your opinion.
Write about
- your own experience of travel.
- the good things and downsides of travelling.
- whether or not you prefer staying at home and watching travel programmes on TV or on the internet.

Write about 120 words. Count your words at the end.

IV. Writing – Set 2

Part 1 – A letter of complaint

You bought a gadget from an online company, but you aren't satisfied with it.
Write an email to the company:
- Say what you bought, when you bought it and how you paid for it.
- Say why you aren't satisfied with it.
- Say what you want the company to do.

The pictures are only examples of gadgets.
Write about 80 words.

Part 2 – A blog entry: the best day in my life

Write a blog about one of the best days in your life.
In your entry describe in detail:
- what happened,
- how you felt,
- why the day was so special.

Write about 120 words.

Mündliche Prüfung

Speaking about yourself

a) Questions + short answers
Answer these questions about yourself.
1 Hello. Can you tell me your name, please, and how you spell it?
2 How are you today?
3 What's the weather like today?
4 How do you come to school every day?
5 How long does it take you?
6 When will you arrive home this afternoon?

b) Questions + longer answers
Give longer answers to these questions.
1 Please tell me something about your family and pets.
2 What sort of physical activity do you like best? Why?
3 Would you like to stay in this town when you leave school? Why (not)?
4 Please tell me something about the TV programmes you like watching.

c) Picture prompt

Talk about the picture.
– What can you see?
– Talk about their feelings.

d) Discussion

In this part of the test you are talking to each other.
Imagine that a group of friends at your school would like to meet when you are free after the end of the school year. Talk to your partner about activities that the group could do.
On your cards there are some ideas, but you can suggest other things too.
Talk to your partner about the pros and cons of some activities and try to agree on three activities which you could suggest to the whole group of friends.
You have about five minutes. Start when you are ready.

Two days in London	Camping on a farm
Hiking in the Alps	Surfing course in Cornwall
A painting course	Weekend in Berlin
Candidate 1	**Candidate 2**
A holiday flat on the Turkish coast — Canoe holiday in Mecklenburg	Rafting in the south of France — Beach holiday in Spain
Anything else?	Anything else?

Schriftliche Prüfung

Bearbeitungszeit: 120 min

I. Listening

Part 1 – Questions 1–4

You will hear four short conversations.
For each question there are three pictures and a short recording.
Choose the correct picture and put a tick (✓) in the box below it.

1 What did the boy have for breakfast?

A ☐

B ☐

C ☐

2 What happened to Megan?

A ☐

B ☐

C ☐

3 What train is the boy running to?

A ☐

B ☐

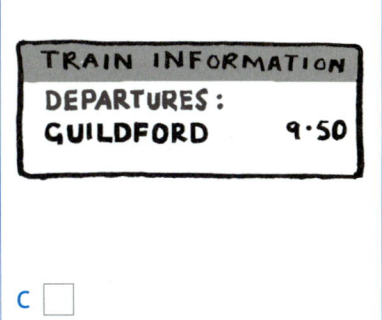
C ☐

4 What has the woman lost?

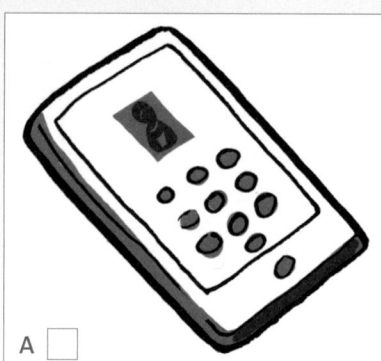
A ☐

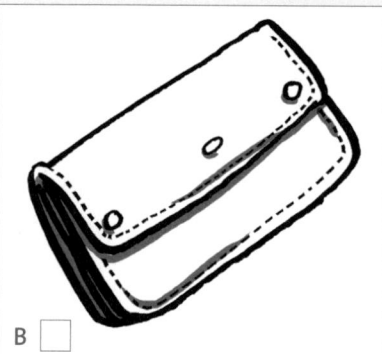
B ☐

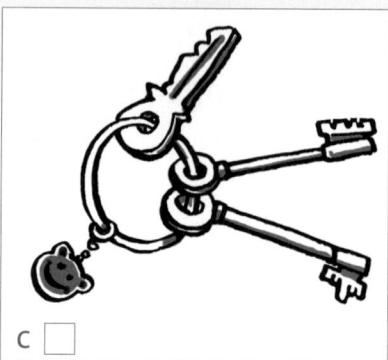
C ☐

 Part 2 – Questions 5–10

First job

Tom is looking for work. Listen to the following conversations at a job fair and then at Tom's first place of work. For questions 5–10 tick (✓) the correct box a), b) or c).
The first question is an example.

0 Tom is looking for …

  a) ☐ evening work.
  b) ✓ part-time work.
  c) ☐ full-time work.

5 The first employer didn't offer Tom a job because …

  a) ☐ Tom had never worked in a cafe before.
  b) ☐ Tom was too young.
  c) ☐ Tom was still a student at school.

6 Linda offered Tom the opportunity to see if he would like the work by …

  a) ☐ working unpaid for a day.
  b) ☐ working paid for a day.
  c) ☐ working paid for two hours.

7 When Linda tells Tom that she wants to talk with him, he feels …

  a) ☐ confident.
  b) ☐ worried.
  c) ☐ happy because he knows that he has worked well.

8 Linda told Tom that she hadn't talked with him much because …

  a) ☐ she had been too busy.
  b) ☐ managers should not talk too much with their workers.
  c) ☐ she had been away.

9 Tom's work in the *Happy Diner* restaurant included preparing food and …

  a) ☐ cleaning the tables.
  b) ☐ taking money.
  c) ☐ washing up.

10 Linda was happy with Tom's work, so she …

  a) ☐ offered him a bonus of £10 a week.
  b) ☐ paid him a single payment of £10.
  c) ☐ said that he might get a £10 bonus in the future.

MUSTERPRÜFUNG 2: Listening

Part 3 – Questions 11–16

Concorde

You are doing a project on special planes, and you hear this radio programme about Concorde. Listen to the programme. Complete the notes by filling the gaps 11–16.
The first question is an example.

Concorde fact file		
Made in Britain and	0	*France*
Top speed:	11	over _____
Fastest time from New York JFK to London Heathrow:	12	_____
Most frequent route:	13	_____
Problems:		a) too noisy
	14	b) _____
	15	c) _____
What happened in July 2000:	16	_____

Part 4 – Questions 17–23

Cricket in India

Look at the seven sentences for this part.
You will hear a radio interview about the sport of cricket and the role of India in the sport.
For questions 17–23 decide whether each sentence is true or false.
Put a tick (✓) in the correct box 'true' or 'false'.
The first question is an example.

		true	false
0	Aarav Malhotra is a sports correspondent in Delhi.	✓	
17	If young children are excluded, then a large majority of all people in the world are football fans.		
18	Cricket is the second most popular sport in the world, by number of fans.		
19	The number of countries in the cricket World Cup rose with every tournament between 2007 and 2015.		
20	India has won the cricket World Cup more often than any other country.		
21	The cricket players who earn most money are Indian and play in India.		
22	Cricket makes so much money in India because the viewing public is so large.		
23	One problem with cricket is that women still do not play the game.		

India's Rohit Sharma during the ICC Champions Trophy in Cardiff Wales (2013)

II. Reading

Part 1 – Questions 1–5

Read the texts below. Then read the statements (1–5).
Decide whether the statements are true or false.
Then tick (✓) the correct box.

Front of House Staff
Ricardo Eatery, Falmouth
£6.50 – £8.00 an hour

We are currently hiring team members to serve customers in our busy restaurant.
Experience preferred, but not essential.
We offer
- excellent tips
- training and development within your chosen field of hospitality
- accommodation on the premises

Please send a copy of your CV and contact telephone number.
Job type: full-time

Lost puppy

Dexter is a small Terrier puppy, last seen near the playground in Ambrose Street on 27th November.

Dexter is very friendly and likes to be patted – but does not always answer to his name.
Please help us find him!
Small financial reward given.

Phone 07998 934 501.
Thank you!

Bike Bag Phone Holder – with rain cover

Three straps will keep the bag firmly in position. APVC screen allows you to operate phone as normal while it is in the case. Headphone extension cable with 3.5 mm jack included.
The bag is available in two sizes and fits most current mobile phones.

Baxter and sons – your local professional plumber

With a response time of within 30–90 minutes in the local area, whenever possible, we are second to none for emergency plumbing services.

Our trained operators provide free quotes and estimates for any plumbing work. No job too small.

We have a no call out charge so you only pay the price we quote.

		true	false
1	Dexter's owner is offering money if you find the puppy.	☐	☐
2	The restaurant will only take people who have worked in a restaurant before.	☐	☐
3	If you take the job at the restaurant you will be able to live there.	☐	☐
4	The plumber will always return your call in less than 90 minutes.	☐	☐
5	When you want to use your phone, you don't have to take it out of the phone holder.	☐	☐

Part 2 – Questions 6–11

Decide which of the different kinds of holidays described in the texts (A–H) is the most suitable for the young people below (6–11).

6	Lounging on a sunny beach is not for me. For me, holidays are a chance to learn more about a place that I have never been to before. I'm a sucker for city centres packed with ancient buildings, monuments and churches, and I love museums and exhibitions. It's not always easy to find people with the same interests because my sort of holiday sounds too 'heavy' for many people. But when I do meet people with similar interests, we have a great time. **Robyn**
7	When I take a break I want to do something active, and preferably outside. I like cycling and I'm a member of a badminton club, but I'm always open to trying out new sports and activities. Having said that, I'm not so keen on camping! But I don't mind shared accommodation, and I like to stay in places with staff with the expertise and equipment to show you how to tackle a new activity. **Paddy**
8	Holidays are for relaxation. I want time for myself, time to touch base and remember who I really am. And for this I need to be in the country, in touch with nature. However, the snag is that I really don't like stretching my legs too much, and find long walks both tiring and boring. I need time for thinking, for reading, and sometimes just to curl up near a warm fire and not have to think of anything. **Robert**
9	When I go on holiday I don't want to spend ages planning things: I want everything to be easy. I want to be lazy, to relax in the sun, and have everything I need within easy reach. I'm not a great swimmer, but sea bathing is a must. And as I'm used to being with lots of people, I don't want my holiday to be too quiet. I like lively places where there's something going on. **Becky**
10	I broke up with my boyfriend a few months ago, so I'll be going on my own and I'll want plenty of opportunities to get chatting with people. I want to go abroad, but I don't really like organizing things, so I like packages in which the travel, accommodation and visits are all included. I'm quite active, but I can't stand loud hotels. I like walking around towns, but I prefer watching people and taking in the atmosphere on my own, rather than having guided tours. **Hannah**
11	Holidays? They're for travelling! I love the freedom to decide where to go. Sometimes I join some friends touring about in their old car, sometimes I prefer to travel on my own. I don't mind how I travel – the important thing for me is to see as many different places as possible. And I don't need expensive accommodation: I have my hike tent and sleeping bag, and don't mind sleeping on the floor if necessary! **Rafi**

A   Come to the Lake District, England's most popular national park, and enjoy England's best hiking country. Mountains, lakes, valleys – this is where you can easily escape the crowds. Charge your batteries as you climb Scafell Pike, England's highest mountain. Experience nature in all its power and glory. Put on your boots, pack your rain clothes just in case, don't forget your map – and choose a hiking route that you'll never, ever forget.

B   Marbella Bella Hotel Review
Large modern hotel located in Marbella, on the sun-drenched Costa del Sol in the south of Spain. 10 minutes from the beach and 5 minutes from the main street with shops, cafes, restaurants, etc. This hotel is for party people, a place to make friends. The rooms are OK: clean and quite big. The pool is nice and big and has plenty of loungers. But be aware that it is often quite noisy as people are coming back from parties all night.

C   Take a holiday in Adventure Land and you'll never regret it. Based near Nottingham, in Robin Hood country, we offer an incredible variety of activities, from boxing to philosophy classes, from rowing to table tennis, from archery to quad driving. Best of all, the price of your holiday includes your accommodation, full use of the surrounding forest area and unlimited access to our Exotic Swimming Paradise – where it never rains, because it is under an enormous glass roof! Easy to book, and great for meeting new people.

D   Join us on a weekend in Prague for culture vultures. Included in the package are the flights to and from any UK airport, full-board accommodation, all entrance fees and – especially – the services of an expert guide on both Saturday and Sunday. After a coach tour of the city on Saturday morning, we'll visit the Castle and the Archbishop's Palace. In the evening we'll attend a concert, ballet or opera. And on the Sunday we've planned a guided tour of the Tyn Church, Bethlehem Chapel and Jewish Cemetery. A great opportunity to uncover the secrets of Prague in the friendly company of like-minded people.

E   Flexibility is the name of the game when you explore Europe with Interrail. You don't have to plan everything in advance – you jump on a train when you want to. Once you have bought your Interrail Pass, all train travel is free. You can for example opt for 5 days of travel within a period of 15 days for 206 euros*, or 7 days of travel within a month for 253 euros*. Or travel every day within a month for 493 euros*. It's up to you. Travel from Finland to Portugal, or from Turkey to Ireland. And remember: if you plan your journey well, you can often spend the night on the train – and avoid the price of a hotel room!   *Prices quoted are for travellers aged up to 27.

F   Visitors come to our monastery in a quiet and beautiful valley in the Yorkshire Dales National Park for a number of different reasons. Some just spend a night, some stay for a week or more. Some just want bed and breakfast accommodation, while others take part in a 'retreat': a time when you can be alone, if you wish, or in a group, enjoying quiet relaxation, appreciating the monastery's gardens in silence or taking part in our daily prayer. There is the opportunity to speak in confidence to our Retreat Director, and to meditate on themes suggested by the Retreat Director. Our visitors regularly report that they feel rested and renewed after a retreat, and fitter for the lives they go back to.

G   Coach trip to the Low Countries. Join us on an 8-day tour of Belgium, Luxemburg and the Netherlands, where you will be free to explore Bruges, Ghent, Brussels, Liège, Luxemburg, Maastricht, Amsterdam and Delft in any way you wish. Your holiday begins with a relaxing overnight boat cruise from Hull to Zeebrugge and finishes with a return overnight cruise back to Hull from Rotterdam. The package includes the ferry, luxury coach travel on the European mainland, and half-board accommodation in 4 or 5 stars hotels (drinks not included). The price does not include your travel to Hull or entrance fees to museums, etc.

H   Situated in the hills of the Yorkshire Moors National Park, Levisham Park Centre provides high quality outdoor learning, with real outdoor activities in the natural environment. Activities include rock climbing, hill walking, camping, sailing, orienteering, canoeing and kayaking, caving, ropes course, gorge walking and mountain biking. Accommodation is in double rooms or 8-bed dormitories. All our trainers are fully qualified and have many years of experience with working with young people in challenging surroundings.

Part 3 – Questions 12–18

Read the text and then tick (✓) the correct statement. There is only one correct solution per statement.

Life in South Africa today

This is a magazine article about life for young South Africans today.

In all countries society is constantly changing, but few countries have changed as radically as South Africa. Before the country's first free elections in 1994, everything in your life depended on the colour of your skin. Under a system called apartheid, black and white people lived in different zones, went to different schools, had different jobs, relaxed on different beaches and even used different public toilets. Black people could not vote, and marriages between black and white people were forbidden. This system led to street protests by the black population, which were violently put down by the forces of the white government. Many unarmed protesters were killed, many more were locked up in prison.

The election of Nelson Mandela, South Africa's first black president, in 1994 changed all that. Apartheid was abolished and all South Africans – black, white and Asian – now enjoy equal rights. The country has eleven official languages (English, Afrikaans and nine African languages), which means that local communities can send their children to schools which teach in their own language. It is this wide range of cultures, languages and ethnic backgrounds, rather than the climate or the sometimes colourful way of dressing, that has led South Africa to be given the nickname of the *Rainbow Nation*.

But changes for the better are coming too slowly for many black South Africans who were born after 1994. The white population (nine percent of the total population) still has a larger proportion of the country's wealth than the black South Africans, who make up 80 percent of the population. True, there is now a small number of black people who have also become rich, but about 54 percent of the black population live in poverty, according to a government report in 2014, compared to 0.8 percent of the white population.

You see this inequality in many of South Africa's primary and secondary schools. Schools in mostly white areas of the country are well equipped, while many schools in mostly black areas have poor facilities – not only too few computers, but maybe only one toilet for 60 students. And schools that teach in one of the nine official African languages often find it difficult to employ teachers who can speak their language.

Life is particularly hard for girls because they suffer the most from violence in the streets. About one third of girls suffer from sexual violence before the age of eighteen. The rates of HIV infections are high, and over 60 percent of the victims are women. Many children have to manage life on their own because their parents die young, and they often have to leave school in order to look after younger brothers and sisters. The children are often terrified of falling ill themselves.

South Africa's economy is now growing by less than two percent a year, which is a lower increase than in the first years of the twenty-first century. This means that the government now has less money to spend on improving schools and social conditions.

South Africa's problems should not be exaggerated. The country has not been destroyed by violence. The economy is the biggest in Africa after Nigeria, and incomes per person are among the highest in Africa. Conditions have improved for most people, and blacks can now go onto beaches and into bars that were once reserved for whites. However, life is still hard for many South Africans. The gap between the standard of living of black and white South Africans is as large as ever, and there is little real mixing of the different populations. So it's not surprising that more and more blacks are becoming impatient for real change.

12 The writer's opinion is that life in South Africa …
- a) ☐ has changed less than in most countries.
- b) ☐ has changed about the same as in most countries.
- c) ☐ has changed more than in most countries.
- d) ☐ has not changed much in the last few years.

13 Under apartheid black people …
- a) ☐ could take part in elections, but couldn't marry white people.
- b) ☐ could take part in elections, but couldn't use the same beaches as white people.
- c) ☐ couldn't take part in elections, but could marry white people.
- d) ☐ couldn't take part in elections and couldn't marry white people.

14 South Africa is sometimes called the *Rainbow Nation* because …
- a) ☐ the country celebrates its multicultural society.
- b) ☐ people wear very colourful clothes.
- c) ☐ it has a climate with a high number of rainbows.
- d) ☐ rainbows are important in traditional stories.

15 The situation today, according to the text, is that …
- a) ☐ black South Africans now have more money than white South Africans.
- b) ☐ about half of black South Africans are poor.
- c) ☐ only 0.8 percent of the white population are still rich.
- d) ☐ most South Africans feel that conditions are changing fast enough.

16 Many South African children live independently and don't go school because …
- a) ☐ this is what their culture expects of them.
- b) ☐ disease has killed their parents.
- c) ☐ many schools don't have enough toilets.
- d) ☐ their parents get work in other countries.

17 In the first years of the twenty-first century the South African government …
- a) ☐ had more money to spend than it did later.
- b) ☐ could not spend as much money as it did later.
- c) ☐ could spend less on schools than today.
- d) ☐ was still trying to enforce apartheid.

18 Today, South Africans …
- a) ☐ have the biggest economy in Africa.
- b) ☐ earn less than in most African countries.
- c) ☐ on the whole enjoy a better life than they did in 1994.
- d) ☐ all have more or less the same standard of living.

Part 4 – Questions 19 – 23

Read the blog and then tick (✓) the correct statement.
There is only one correct solution per statement.

My three favourite tourist attractions in Brighton

The sun is shining, the beach is busy – but the sea ... is too cold for swimming. That's why Brighton has always provided attractions on land, and with this first attraction on my list, the British Airways i360, which opened in August 2016, Brighton hopes to keep its 11 million visitors coming well into the future.

So what is the British Airways i360? Imagine a narrow concrete tower, 162 metres high. You travel up the tower in a large cabin or capsule that glides up the outside of the tower. 200 people have space in the cabin: they can move around in it and enjoy a 360-degree view of the town below, with the sea on one side, and the green hills of the Sussex countryside on the other.

Of course you pay to travel slowly up the tower, enjoy the view from the top, and travel slowly down again. Rides cost £15 for tourists and £7.50 for residents. The aim of these prices is to attract not only tourists, but also people who live in Brighton.

The second attraction on my list is a strange, exotic-looking building in a park with exotic trees and plants, with lots of towers and five onion-shaped domes that don't look English at all. In fact, this building looks like a palace in a child's book of fairy tales. Well, it is a palace, and it's real. It was built between 1815 and 1822 for the son of the king of England, a prince called George. Prince George did not like working, and found London too serious – he preferred dancing and drinking and having expensive parties with his friends. So the palace – called the Royal Pavilion – was built to give Prince George a place where he could escape life in boring London.

Today the palace is open to the public. You walk through the living rooms, bedrooms, music rooms and dining hall of George and his rich friends, but also

The Royal Pavilion

through the kitchens where the servants prepared the food and did the washing up. It's the contrast between these two lifestyles that makes a visit so special. Entrance fees are £12.30 for adults, and £6.90 for children under 15.

Third on my list is an underground attraction – and the smell is awful! That's because I'm in a tunnel of the Brighton sewers. The sewers are the tunnels that carry the dirty water from Brighton's streets, but also from the kitchens, bathrooms and toilets.

Now I realize that sewers are a strange place for a visit, but you see these tunnels are very old. They were built in 1860 – before that, this water was just thrown into the streets. The result was that people fell ill, or even died of disease. These tunnels were built to make Brighton safer and healthier for everybody – and they were a big success. Fewer people died of cholera and other terrible diseases.

Of course, all towns have sewers now – but not many have sewers that you can visit. Perhaps because not many people want to visit sewers ... But you'd be surprised. The visits are so popular that you have to book in advance. They cost £12 for adults and £6 for children. The minimum age of admission is eleven.

		true	false	line(s)
19	In the British Airways i360, tourists climb the steps of a tower to enjoy a view from an altitude of 162 metres.	☐	☐	
20	Prices for the British Airways i360 are lower for the local population.	☐	☐	
21	The Royal Pavilion is a palace that was built for a king of England.	☐	☐	
22	After the Brighton Sewers were built, nobody died of cholera or other awful diseases.	☐	☐	
23	You have to order your tickets for a tour of the Brighton Sewers before you visit.	☐	☐	

III. Mediating

Zwei syrische Familien sind in deinem Dorf außerhalb von Hannover untergebracht. Vor dem Jugendklub im Dorf triffst du einen Jungen aus einer der Familien. Er kommt mit dir rein und möchte an der Rezeption ein paar Fragen stellen. Er spricht aber kein Deutsch und die Sekretärin traut sich nicht, Englisch zu reden. Also bietest du an, zu vermitteln.

Junge Are there any courses here to help people from other countries learn German?

You (1) _____

Sekretärin Nein, das haben wir leider nicht. Unser Dorf ist dafür zu klein. Aber solche Kurse gibt es auf jeden Fall in Hannover.

You (2) _____

Junge I don't know Hannover very well. Where can I find information about courses to learn German?

You (3) _____

Sekretärin Ich weiß es nicht genau. Aber man könnte sich zum Beispiel beim Rathaus erkundigen.

You (4) _____

Sekretärin Ach, da mir fällt etwas ein: Wir haben hier irgendwo eine Broschüre über eine Beratungsstelle, die vielleicht nützlich wäre. Ich schaue mal nach ... Ja, hier ist eine. Bitte schön. Nimm sie gerne mit.

You (5) _____

Junge Oh, thank you very much. Err ... *Dankeschön*. It's really kind of the lady, but I'm sorry, I can't read the brochure. Can you tell me how this place can help us and when it's open?

Schau dir die Broschüre (auf S. 65) an und mache zwei Vorschläge.

You (6/7) _____

_____

Kontakt- und Beratungsstellen

Wir haben drei Kontakt- und Beratungsstellen in Hannover. Der engagierte Einsatz unserer ehrenamtlichen Mitarbeiter ermöglicht das Angebot in Hannover-Mitte und Hannover Nordstadt an 365 Tagen im Jahr. Die Stelle in Ricklingen ist an jedem Werktag geöffnet.

Die Kontakt- und Beratungsstellen sind ein offenes Angebot, und gerade diese Offenheit macht es für viele Menschen leichter, den Zugang zu uns zu finden. Ganz wichtig ist der Mittagstisch, der außer in Ricklingen an jedem Werktag angeboten wird. Hier wird der erste Kontakt zu unseren Mitarbeitern und zu anderen Besuchern schnell und informell gemacht, zu weiteren Gesprächen und Hilfen ist es dann nur ein kleiner Schritt. In der Beratung findet jeder Verständnis, erhält Rat und Information. In der Kontakt- und Beratungsstelle Ricklingen gibt es spezielle Angebote für Menschen mit Migrationshintergrund. Die Beratung kann in türkischer, arabischer und serbischer Sprache erfolgen.

Menschen mit psychischer Erkrankung und Sucht finden in all unseren Kontakt- und Beratungsstellen einen Ansprechpartner.

Und selbstverständlich kommen wir zu den Menschen nach Hause, die selbst nicht zu uns kommen können, aber trotzdem Hilfe möchten. Wir bieten kurzfristige und kostenlose Hausbesuche zur Beratung oder Betreuung an. Ein Anruf genügt. Unsere besuchenden Helfer durchbrechen den Kreis der Isolation.

IV. Writing – Set 1

Part 1 – Giving information

Your Scottish exchange partner has sent you photos of her school and has asked you to write something about your school or German schools in general.
Write about 50 words. Count your words.

Part 2 – Writing about a problem

It's winter, and yesterday it wasn't easy to get to school. Write a short email to an English friend. Tell him or her why it was difficult to get to school. Write about 50 words. Count your words.
The pictures are <u>only examples</u> of things that went wrong.

Part 3 – An online discussion

An online magazine has opened a discussion on the following topic:
We all know that we should do more sport. So why don't we do it?

Write an entry on this discussion giving your opinion.
Write about • why sport is important.
• your own experience of different sports.
• your opinion on the question in the title.

Write about 120 words. Count your words at the end.

V. Writing – Set 2

Part 1 – A letter to a town council

You have spent a week in an English family and had a great time.
But there was one big problem: cycling in town was dangerous because there were very few cycle lanes on the roads.
Before you return to Germany, you decide to write to the town council about this issue.

- Describe what made cycling dangerous in town.
- Compare your experiences with cycling in your home town in Germany.
- Suggest what the town council could do to help cyclists.

Write about 80 words. Count your words.
The pictures are only examples.

Part 2 – A competition

My favourite of all places

You enter a competition with a prize of 200 euros. To win the competition, you have to write about a place and explain why it is your favourite place. It can be a region, a town, or a place in town or in the country.

In your entry you have to:
- say what the place is and describe it,
- write about a time when you went there or heard about it,
- explain why it means so much to you.

Write about 120 words.

Mündliche Prüfung

Speaking about yourself

a) Questions + short answers
   Answer these questions about yourself.
   1 Hello. How are you feeling?
   2 Can you tell me your name, please?
   3 And can you please tell me what the time is?
   4 How many brothers and sisters do you have?
   5 What's your favourite sport?
   6 What day of the week is it tomorrow?

b) Questions + longer answers
   Give longer answers to these questions.
   1 Please tell me something about the house or flat in which you live.
   2 What do you usually do in the summer holidays?
   3 What is your favourite subject at school? Why?
   4 Do you like the town or village in which you live? Why (not)?

c) Picture prompt

Talk about the picture.
– What can you see?
– Talk about his feelings.

d) Discussion

> In this part of the test you are talking to each other.
> Students in your partner school in Wales want to hear what you think about your town and what it could do to improve life for young people.
> Talk to each other about what is good for young people in your town and what could be better. Try to agree on three ideas to make things better.
> There are some topics on your cards, but you can suggest other things too.
> You have about five minutes. Start when you are ready.

Candidate 1
- Cycle lanes
- Sports centres
- Cost of renting a flat
- College choices when you leave school
- Jobs for young people
- Any more ideas?

Candidate 2
- Bus travel for young people
- Youth clubs
- Wi-fi in town
- Rollerblading parks
- Cinema
- Any more ideas?

Schriftliche Prüfung

Bearbeitungszeit: 120 min

I. Listening

Part 1 – Questions 1–4

You will hear four short conversations.
For each question there are three pictures and a short recording.
Choose the correct picture and put a tick in the box below it.

1 What made a specially good impression at the grand dinner?

2 What's the weather forecast for Saturday afternoon?

3 What does the boy want for his room?

 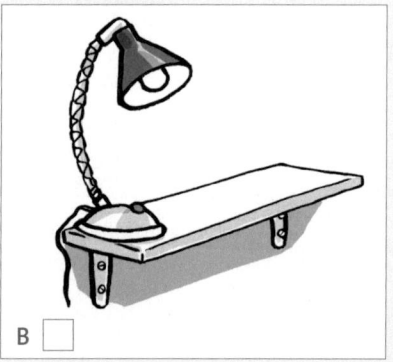 

4 What was the first thing that went wrong?

A ☐

B ☐

C ☐

Part 2 – Questions 5–10

A presentation about Wales

Listen to four students in the USA. They are giving a presentation about Wales.
For questions 5–10 tick (✓) the correct box a), b) or c).
The first question is an example.

0 Welsh MPs sit in the Houses of Parliament in …
- a) ☐ Edinburgh.
- b) ☐ Dublin.
- c) ✓ London.

5 In the EURO 2016 football championship …
- a) ☐ Wales won against England.
- b) ☐ Wales reached the semi-finals.
- c) ☐ Wales did better than Germany.

6 The Welsh language is …
- a) ☐ a dialect of English.
- b) ☐ different from English, but with many similarities.
- c) ☐ not like English at all.

7 The Welsh language is …
- a) ☐ mainly spoken in Brittany in the north-west of France.
- b) ☐ widely spoken all over Wales.
- c) ☐ only spoken by a minority of people in Wales.

8 In the centre of Wales you'll find …
- a) ☐ lots of farm animals.
- b) ☐ rather flat countryside.
- c) ☐ the larger towns of Wales.

9 Most of the castles in Wales …
- a) ☐ were built by a Welsh king to protect Wales from the English.
- b) ☐ were built by an English king to help him rule the people of Wales.
- c) ☐ have been completely destroyed.

10 The south of Wales …
- a) ☐ produces lots of coal.
- b) ☐ has few people because so many have emigrated to Australia.
- c) ☐ has the most people in Wales.

Part 3 – Questions 11–17

St Kilda

You have been listening to a series of radio programmes about the UNESCO World Heritage sites in Britain. Here is the last programme in the series.
Listen to the programme.
Complete the notes by filling the gaps 11–17.
The first question is an example.

St Kilda – a UNESCO World Heritage site		
Distance away from Scotland:	0	*100 miles*
For food people on St Kilda	11	
	12	
What carried the post to Scotland?	13	
Reasons why the population of St Kilda fell:	14	
	15	
In 1930	16	the people of St Kilda
Visitors to St Kilda	17	can stay in

Part 4 – Questions 18–25

The D of E *expedition*

Look at the seven sentences for this part.
You will hear part of a live reading from *Dreamings*, a book about a girl's adventurous summer in Britain. In this excerpt, Keira is on an expedition with her friends. For questions 18–25 decide whether each sentence is true or false.
Put a tick in the correct box 'true' or 'false'.
The first question is an example.

		true	false
0	At the beginning of the story, Keira didn't want to do anything.	✓	
18	The Queen's husband, The Duke of Edinburgh, set up the challenge for young people.		
19	A bronze award involves volunteering, a new sport or physical activity, a skill and a two-day expedition.		
20	A silver award involves a longer expedition, but no volunteering.		
21	On the first day the four friends in the story got lost.		
22	The problem during the night was that the ground was hard.		
23	On the second day Ibrahim fell and hurt himself.		
24	Keira wasn't tired at the end of the second day, but very thirsty.		
25	At the end Keira doesn't know if she has the strength to continue.		

II. Reading

Part 1 – Questions 1–5

Read the texts below. Then read the statements (1–5).
Decide whether the statements are true or false.
Then tick (✓) the correct box.

St Bede Centre, Kirkpatrick Road Jarrow
25th January, 7.30 pm–10 pm

Our traditional community Ceilidh to celebrate Burns Night

Scottish dancing to the music of our very own live band. No experience needed: tuition for the dances given on the night. Everyone welcome to dance or listen to the music. Admission: adult £3, child £1 (under 8 years with adult please). Pay at the door.

Ideal for long road journeys!

Our ingeniously-designed, multi-pocket, seatback-hanging Orgy-Organizer effortlessly stores toys, snacks, drinks, phones, tablets, books, magazines, and much more.

Makes efficient use of the back of the passenger seat. Keeps your car tidy and helps you to find things easily.

Dimensions: 36.5 x 34 cm

Weight: 480 g

Material: waterproof acrylic

£12.99 + free delivery in mainland Britain

Newspaper delivery person required. Must be local to the Wincheap area of Canterbury.

Deliveries are Mon–Sat. Rounds take about 25 minutes per day, and we'll pay you from £15.50 per weekly round.

Sunday-only rounds also available at £3 per round (again about 20 minutes per round).

Please apply online for further details.

Canterbury Chronicle: Delivering newspapers within the Canterbury Area.

Cute **baby tortoises** for sale for £100 each. Most are probably female, but some may be male. These pets are unsuitable for young children as they are considered to be an endangered species.

I can provide the necessary housing for summer and winter, including UVB lighting, for an extra charge – everything you need to look after a baby tortoise.

With proper care and correct feeding, tortoises can grow to be 100 years old – so please only buy one if you want to keep it for a long time!

		true	false
1	The Orgy-Organizer is a product to put in a car.	☐	☐
2	The tortoises would make a great present for young girls and boys because they live for a very long time.	☐	☐
3	The housing and lighting for the tortoises are included in the price of the animals.	☐	☐
4	If you deliver newspapers for the Canterbury Chronicle, you'll earn £15.50 for working 25 minutes on five days a week.	☐	☐
5	People can teach you to dance at the Ceilidh if you need help.	☐	☐

Part 2 – Questions 6–11

The young people below (6–11) are all looking for a job for the summer.
Decide which of the different jobs (A–H) is the most suitable for each person.

6		Kylie (18) has never been afraid to take up causes whether they were popular or not. She is a passionate vegan, for example, partly for health reasons, but also as an expression of her consideration for the environment and for the welfare of animals. She once worked in a meat-packing factory – never again! Kylie is, to be honest, not always the most patient of people, but she is always ready to argue for her case and persuade people of her convictions.
7		Abdul (18) grew up in Afghanistan, in a house surrounded by plants and flowers, and he has always had a love of nature. Since arriving in Britain, he has read up about British wildlife, and his aim is to study botany at a university. For the summer he wants a full-time job with work outside in a park or garden. He doesn't mind working outside in the rain.
8		Simona's family is originally from Spain, although she has lived in Sheffield for five years now and speaks English with a nice Yorkshire accent. In Year 11 she did her work experience in a kindergarten. She enjoyed working with children and would like to do that again in her summer job, especially if she could combine it with doing something sporty, because she is something of a sports fanatic.
9		Andy (18) is a good all-rounder, good at sport, interested in science, and a keen guitarist. And he manages all that even though he is taking driving lessons with the aim of taking his test in October. For the summer, Andy is looking for a job in the social work or care for the elderly sector. Andy is patient and considerate, and has experience of looking after his grandpa, so he has some informal experience.

10		Jessica is an open, friendly student who gets on well with most of the students in her year. She is tidy and likes to be well dressed, and her presentations are always especially well prepared. Her aim is to take up a career in marketing, where she hopes to do publicity for some high-profile customers. She has no special preference for a summer job, although she does not like outdoor work. She is very flexible, and rather enjoys the excitement of not knowing what each day will bring.
11		Yana (18) has her idea of an ideal afternoon: being outside in the hills, by a river or waterfall, doing her favourite hobby – photography. Mind you, she likes being indoors doing photography too, taking portraits of her friends and family. She had always been fascinated by this activity, and when she leaves school she hopes to be able to widen her repertoire by focusing on photography at college.

A **Grasper Plc.** We are currently recruiting for a door-to-door charity fundraiser to raise money for the British Pony Trust. This is a great opportunity to work on behalf of an organization that looks after ponies across the UK. We will train you in your role and prepare you for what you can expect on the doorstep. You will be part of a team, with other members also working in your area. This is a job for a caring person with a good command of English. All fundraisers must be over 18 years of age.

B **The Sheffield Parks Division** needs helpers for the current restoration of three Victorian parks across the city. Your task will be to support our team of professional botanists and park keepers, and the majority of your work will be outside. It will involve planting trees and flowers, weeding, digging, and similar tasks. These part-time jobs, paid at a rate of £8.50 an hour, will be available from the beginning of May to the end of September.

C Here at **GreatCare UK** we provide a range of home services for elderly people who need help in order to be able to continue to live in their own homes. This might include washing, dressing, preparing a simple meal, or simply sitting down to chat. Our assistants cover a considerable area of Sheffield and frequently need to drive from one customer to the next. A driving licence is therefore essential, and we pay you for your travel time. Applicants must be 18 or over. Please apply and supply a CV online.

D **Premium Hospitality** Do you fancy working with film and music stars in some of the best venues in town? Then look no further. We specialise in hospitality at concerts, theatre, film premieres and major sports events, so this is a unique opportunity to see what goes on backstage at many of Sheffield's biggest and most star-studded events. As a member of our team of waiters and bar staff you will help us look after our VIPs and their guests. All we ask is that you are able to work at short notice, as we often do not know what our requirements are till the morning of the event. In return we'll look after you while you work with us, with full training and good rates of pay.

E **Clovis** is a registered charity that offers work to people including people with learning disabilities. We grow and sell a wide range of seasonal organic fruit, vegetables and plants in pots including bedding plants, cottage garden perennials and herbs. For the coming months we have full-time work available maintaining churchyards and restoring and tidying individuals' gardens. Please phone for details.

F **PicPac** Be that person that captures and records amazing moments! We work in the leisure, theme park and tourist industries, and our aim is to allow visitors to keep their memories and share them with friends, family and the world. We offer a wide choice of formats for memorable pictures, whether digitally, in print, on mugs and plates, on T-shirts, etc. We are always on the lookout for talent and people who are able to take dramatic pictures of happy people.

G Peak District Activity Centres Our Activity Assistants help our Activity Instructors to train groups of children in outdoor activities such as abseiling, canoeing, kayaking, rock-climbing, etc. They help with the evening entertainment and are prepared to do other tasks including cleaning and serving meals. We are ideally looking for people who can commit to full-time work and have a NGB qualification such as BC 2*/3*/4* Canoe and/or Kayak. But if you don't have a qualification yet, don't worry! Our non-qualified assistants receive training and are not required to take full responsibility for activities.

H The lives of so many sick and aged people can be transformed by providing them with just an hour or two of help a day. That is our aim here at **LocalSocial**. With funds from local sponsors (mainly large companies), we pay for our workers to visit people near to where they live, and to help with whatever needs doing. It could be just helping people to go to the local shop, it could be providing them with company over a cup of tea. If you believe that everybody deserves an independent life, this is the job for you.

Part 3 – Questions 12–16

This article is from a British fitness and health magazine.
Read the text and then tick (✓) the correct statement.
There is only one correct solution per statement.

Good health in Australia?

Sport, health and Australia seem to go together like bread, butter and jam. Australians have long been stars in rugby, cricket, tennis and sailing; and though Australia only won 35 medals at the 2012 London Olympics, this figure put them way ahead of Britain, Germany or the United States in terms of medals per head of population.

Search Australia's TV channels and slim, healthy individuals will beam at you from the screen, and not only in the adverts. Reality TV shows like *Bondi Beach* and *Surf Patrol* feature the work of volunteer life-savers on Australia's beaches. These men and women, who risk their lives while saving others from drowning and deal with dangers that range from sharks in the sea to thieves on the beach, have one thing in common: they are slim, healthy and agile.

No wonder Australia is such a popular destination for emigrants from Europe. Over 200,000 Brits emigrated to Australia between 2010 and 2015 – three times more than to the USA, the second most popular destination for British emigrants. And the emigrants' happy stories of sunshine, barbecues, surfing, snorkelling and beach volleyball contrast with our indoor existence back in the UK. The Australian sun, we think, encourages Australians to keep fit; our dismal weather gives us a good excuse to watch TV, reach for the comfort food and put on weight.

And yet the reality is different. Australia is in fact experiencing an explosion in obesity rates. In today's obesity rankings, Australia is ahead of France and Germany. The reasons for the problem lie in diet and a general lack of exercise. While almost half of all Australians consume the amount of fruit recommended in the national guidelines, only 7 % meet the target for vegetables. And while just over half of all Aus-

tralians take part in 150 minutes of moderate physical activity per week, as recommended (or 75 minutes of vigorous activity), just under half do not. This includes almost 15% who confess to doing no physical activity at all – and these figures exclude those over 64 years of age.

Australia is of course by no means alone with this problem. It is a feature of modern life in many countries, and not only the wealthiest, for developing nations account for more than half of the world's obese population. And no country anywhere in the world has yet found a way of reducing its obesity rates. However, the huge rise comes as a particularly nasty surprise in Australia because it contrasts so starkly with the self-image of fitness and health. In future, it will be more and more difficult for the makers of the holiday brochures and TV series to find the slim and healthy Australians for their holiday photos and TV series.

12 At the London Olympics in 2012 Australia won ...
- a) ☐ more medals than ever before.
- b) ☐ the most medals since 1992.
- c) ☐ more medals than in 1992.
- d) ☐ more medals than Germany or the UK per person in the country.

13 The main characters in the TV series *Bondi Beach* and *Surf Patrol* ...
- a) ☐ are professional life-savers.
- b) ☐ are in good physical condition.
- c) ☐ sometimes steal things on the beach.
- d) ☐ face few dangers in their work.

14 When emigrants to Australia contact their families in Britain they ...
- a) ☐ say that they sit at home and put on weight.
- b) ☐ give a positive picture of Australia.
- c) ☐ say that they are very fit.
- d) ☐ say that they miss British television.

15 According to the figures in the text, one of the problems is that ...
- a) ☐ hardly any Australians do the recommended amount of exercise per week.
- b) ☐ Australians eat too much meat.
- c) ☐ only a small minority of Australians eat enough vegetables.
- d) ☐ most Australians never do any physical activity.

16 The rates of obesity ...
- a) ☐ are worse in Australia than in any other country.
- b) ☐ have been reversed in many countries of the world.
- c) ☐ are only a problem of the richer countries in the world.
- d) ☐ don't conform to the common view of Australia.

Part 4 – Questions 17–21

Read the online news article and then tick (✓) the correct statement.
There is only one correct solution per statement.

The Mousetrap

Most plays and shows run for a few weeks, some for a few months. But when *The Mousetrap*, a murder mystery play by Agatha Christie, was put on for the 25,000th time in 2012, it had already been running for 60 years. And the play is still performed today, six days a week, with two shows on Tuesdays and Saturdays, making it the longest-running play in the world.

What's more, if you try to book, you may well find that you can't, because tickets have already sold out. For the fact is that this play has become a London tourist attraction in its own right, and a firm fixture on many tours of foreign tourists to Britain, as much as watching the changing of the guards outside Buckingham Palace.

Agatha Christie actually wrote *The Mousetrap* as a radio play in 1947. Then, when it was performed on stage in Nottingham, the theatre critics in many newspapers were dismissive. Agatha Christie herself thought it would run for eight months. But the theatre-goers proved them all wrong.

Of course, the actors in the play have changed over the years. One estimate is that 400 different actors have acted in *The Mousetrap* over the years. One actor, Natasha Rickman, played the very same role that her mother had played many years before!

Of course, being a murder mystery, everybody wants to know who commits the crime: that, after all, is the point of the play. So given that nearly eleven million people have watched the play, you might have thought the secret would by now be common knowledge. But at the end of every show, the members of the audience are asked not to reveal the secret or to share it on social media. And the impressive thing is that, by and large, the secret has been kept. Agatha Christie herself helped to keep the secret by making sure that the play has not been published as a book in the UK, and the play has never been made into a film.

		true	false	line(s)
17	The first stage performance of *The Mousetrap* was in 1952.	☐	☐	_____
18	*The Mousetrap* is popular with English tourists, but not with tourists from abroad because of the language problem.	☐	☐	_____
19	Theatre critics loved *The Mousetrap* from the very beginning.	☐	☐	_____
20	Natasha Rickman and her mother both appeared on stage together in a performance of *The Mousetrap*.	☐	☐	_____
21	The majority of people who have seen *The Mousetrap* have not told their friends who is the murderer.	☐	☐	_____

III. Mediating

Julian, ein Schulkamerad von dir, zieht mit seiner Familie demnächst nach Leeds in Großbritannien. Julian spielt gern Trompete und sucht Möglichkeiten, in Leeds weiter Trompete spielen zu können. Du hast im Internet folgende Informationen gefunden (siehe S. 77). Da Julian Schwierigkeiten hat, die Informationen zu verstehen, bietest du an, ihm dabei zu helfen.

Julian Was für ein Niveau muss man haben, um dort mitspielen zu dürfen?

Du (1) _____

Julian Wann treffen die Orchester zusammen?

Du (2) _____

Julian Was kostet das denn?

Du (3) _____

Julian Heftig! Das ist ganz schön teuer! Gibt es keine Ermäßigungen?

Du (4) _____

Julian Das wäre doch vielleicht was.

Julian hat aber noch weitere Fragen, und bittet dich, den Jugendorchestern in Leeds eine Mail zu schicken, um Folgendes zu klären. Julian möchte wissen, ob es bei den Orchestern eine Altersbegrenzung gibt. Und da es dauern könnte, bis das Gepäck von Julians Familie in Leeds ankommt, wäre es möglich, dass er in der Zwischenzeit ein Musikinstrument zum Üben ausleihen könnte? Außerdem sollst du noch herausfinden, ob die Orchester für ein bestimmtes Konzert proben und ob es etwas ausmacht, wenn Julian noch nicht gut Englisch sprechen kann.

Formuliere die Fragen, die du im Auftrag vom Julian in der Mail stellen willst.

Du (5) _____

Du (6) _____

Du (7) _____

Du (8) _____

Six Youth Orchestras in Leeds!

The Leeds Youth Orchestras are open to all young musicians and cater for all levels of experience. We have six different orchestras, meaning that players of all abilities have a great opportunity to make music with people who are of much the same ability as they are.

Our orchestras meet on Saturday mornings from 10 am to 12.30 and additionally on three days of the week in the school holidays at Easter, in summer and at Christmas. We are fortunate to be able to make use of great facilities at the University of Leeds.

We have an excellent team of professional musicians who lead the sessions and conduct to a very high standard.

The sessions cost £50 per day (or £45 per day for early applications). However, we are keen to make music possible for as many young musicians as possible and therefore offer some assistance with course fees to families facing financial difficulties. Please apply for this help in the appropriate section of the application form.

To apply, simply download and complete our application form. Applications are dealt with on a first-come, first-served basis, so do apply as early as possible.

IV. Writing – Set 1

Part 1 – Answering a letter

Your uncle George, who lives in Belfast, Northern Ireland, has sent you this birthday card.

Happy Birthday!

I really did not know what to buy you as a birthday present.

So here are 50 euros for you. Have fun – and please write to me and tell me how you spent them.

George

Write an e-mail back telling your uncle how you spent the money.
Write about 50 words. Count your words.

Part 2 – A review for a hotel

On a holiday in Italy you stayed in the Hotel Adria.
Write a review of the hotel for an online comparison website.
You can decide if the hotel was very good or very bad.
You can write about things like the food, the rooms, the beach – or you can use your own ideas.
Write about 50 words.

Part 3 – A blog

Social media and the generations

You have found the following blog entry:
Are social media dividing the generations?
Young people can't live without social media, but many older people don't use them as much, or not at all. Is this making relations between the generations more difficult?

Write an entry on this blog giving your opinion. Write about
- your personal experience with social media,
- your experience of how older people use (or don't use) social media,
- whether or not you think that social media are causing problems between the generations.

Write about 120 words. Count your words at the end.

IV. Writing – Set 2

Part 1 – An application to take part in an event

During a stay in England you read this brochure about a marathon run.

Join us on Saturday 20th May in the
Great Midlands Run

Run any distance from 1 to 20 miles, and it's free!
Please register online – only registered runners can take part.

You're a keen runner and would like to take part in the run.
The online application form has the following section:

Please tell us
- *why you want to run*
- *your experience of running*
- *how you heard about the run*
- *how you will get to the starting point (public transport, …?)*

Do you have any questions about the run?

Write your answer and ask some questions about the run.
Write about 80 words. Count your words.

Part 2 – A picture story

Write a story based on the pictures above. Give it a suitable title and an ending.
Write about 120 words. Count your words.

Übersicht über die Aufgaben zum Hörverstehen

Die Tonaufnahmen (MP3-Dateien) und die Hörtexte findest du online unter www.scook.de.
Deinen persönlichen Zugangscode findest du auf Seite 1 deines Abschlussprüfungstrainers.

Track	Kapitel	Titel	Seite
1	Training Section	Sound sequence audio prompt	10
2	Training Section	Olivia and Dad	15
3	Training Section	Tim's visit to Krakow	15
4	Training Section	Calgary's skyways (Part 1)	16
5	Training Section	Calgary's skyways (Part 2)	17
6	Training Section	The Tour de Yorkshire	17
7	Training Section	Bob Marley	18
8	Training Section	Top of the Rock	19
9	Musterprüfung 1	Where did Sabrina go last weekend?	42
10	Musterprüfung 1	What activity will Noah and his friends probably do at the school fair?	42
11	Musterprüfung 1	When should Mrs Taylor be at the dentist?	42
12	Musterprüfung 1	Where's the post office?	43
13	Musterprüfung 1	Bo-Kaap – a special district in Cape Town	43
14	Musterprüfung 1	A presentation about William Shakespeare	44
15	Musterprüfung 1	A great language experience	44
16	Musterprüfung 2	What did the boy have for breakfast?	55
17	Musterprüfung 2	What happened to Megan?	55
18	Musterprüfung 2	What train is the boy running to?	55
19	Musterprüfung 2	What has the woman lost?	56
20	Musterprüfung 2	First job	56
21	Musterprüfung 2	Concorde	57
22	Musterprüfung 2	Cricket in India	57
23	Musterprüfung 3	What made a specially good impression at the grand dinner?	68
24	Musterprüfung 3	What's the weather forecast for Saturday afternoon?	68
25	Musterprüfung 3	What does the boy want for his room?	68
26	Musterprüfung 3	What was the first thing that went wrong?	69
27	Musterprüfung 3	A presentation about Wales	69
28	Musterprüfung 3	St Kilda	70
29	Musterprüfung 3	The D of E expedition	70
30	Urheberrechtserklärung		

Studio: Clarity Studio Berlin
Regie und Aufnahmeleitung: Christian Schmitz
Tontechnik: Christian Marx, Pascal Thinius